B.R. Ambedkar, Economic Development and Dalits in Post-Independence India

This book examines the work of the economist B.R. Ambedkar, focusing on his economic ideas within the context of post-Independence India. It also studies the socio-economic status of Dalits in the country, focusing on Ambedkar's views on inclusive and equitable growth.

The volume:

- Focuses on the economic writings of Ambedkar and looks at his views on caste and its economic implications, monetary and fiscal systems, as well as exchange rate and trade;
- Discusses issues like land reforms and agrarian change, poverty, higher education and human rights from a Dalit perspective;
- Examines the relevance of Ambedkar's economic ideas for contemporary India.

Drawing on interdisciplinary research methods, this book will be of great interest to scholars and researchers of economics, political science, development studies, history, human rights, and South Asian studies.

Prof. Gummadi Nancharaiah was ICSSR National Fellow during 2015–2017 at the School of Economics, University of Hyderabad, India. He has taught Post-Graduate students during the last 45 years at different universities. He was the Dean of School of Economics, University of Hyderabad for 2.5 years (2012–2015). He was the Vice-Chancellor of Babasaheb Bhimrao Ambedkar Central University, Lucknow for five years (2002–2007). He was a Fulbright scholar under the Indo-US Exchange Programme and worked at University of California, Berkeley, USA in 1990. He is the author of *Land and Caste* (1988) and the editor of *Economic Reforms and Rural Development in India* (2003). He was a member of both the Agriculture Commission appointed by Government of Andhra Pradesh (2004) and the High Level Committee constituted by the Ministry of Consumer Affairs, Food and Public Distribution (MCAFPD), Government of India, for restructuring the Food Corporation of India during 2014–2015. He was the Chairman, IV State Finance Commission, Government of Andhra Pradesh for about two years during February 2018 to December 2019.

B.R. Ambedkar, Economic Development and Dalits in Post-Independence India

Gummadi Nancharaiah

Routledge
Taylor & Francis Group
LONDON AND NEW YORK

First published 2022
by Routledge
2 Park Square, Milton Park, Abingdon, Oxon OX14 4RN

and by Routledge
605 Third Avenue, New York, NY 10158

Routledge is an imprint of the Taylor & Francis Group, an informa business

British Library Cataloguing-in-Publication Data
A catalogue record for this book is available from the British Library

Library of Congress Cataloging-in-Publication Data
A catalog record has been requested for this book

ISBN: 978-0-367-64305-8 (hbk)
ISBN: 978-0-367-70582-4 (pbk)
ISBN: 978-1-003-14705-3 (ebk)

DOI: 10.4324/9781003147053

Typeset in Sabon
by SPi Technologies India Pvt Ltd (Straive)

Contents

Tables

Preface

Dr. Ambedkar believed that the state had a crucial role to play in restructuring society under democratic polity and the foundations of democracy would be feeble and shaky if there is no social and economic democracy consistent with political democracy. Dr. Ambedkar opined that existing social and economic institutions, particularly the caste and land tenure system in India, were not conducive for accelerating economic development with social justice and emphasised the need for removing social and economic inequalities as a precondition for a stable democracy and rapid economic development with justice.

After the attainment of Independence, India adopted its national economic policy, with the primary objective of growth with Justice. Self-reliance was one of the important objectives of planning, in addition to the expansion of employment and the removal of poverty. India, like other developing countries, had given priority to import substitution as an effective means of industrialisation. The state was expected to steer the engine of growth and public sector was assigned a crucial role in the process of industrial development. All basic and heavy industries were supposed to be under the control of the public sector. The emphasis was more on aid than on exports. But by the mid-1960s, the problem of foreign exchange became very acute due to drought and the war with Pakistan. The policy was changed to export promotion while continuing import substitution, which has been viewed synonymously as self-reliance. Then several measures to boost exports had been initiated by the Government of India in the form of subsidies to exports and the rupee was devalued by about 57.5% in June 1966. Despite various incentives given to the exporting industry and protection to the import-competing industry in the form of tariffs and other controls on imports during the period 1961–1991, there was a negative trade gap which constituted about 3% of GDP on average. The balance of payments problem, which became very serious in 1991, and also the fallout from the Gulf War, led to the country experiencing what became known as the 1991 economic crisis. Since 1991, the economic policy of India has been liberalised, with the emphasis on privatisation and globalisation. There has been a shift in the Indian economic policy from a state-oriented development strategy to market-oriented development, leaving decisions of production and distribution to market signals. But this new economic policy became controversial as it failed at the global level, particularly in case of some Latin American and African countries.

In this context, the views of Dr. Ambedkar on various aspects of the Indian economy merit serious discussion. An attempt is made in this book to analyse Dr. Ambedkar's views on caste and its economic implications, monetary and fiscal systems, exchange rate and trade, Indian agriculture, education, and his plan of economic development and it also examines their relevance for contemporary India.

The required information is drawn from various works of Dr. Ambedkar - (1) Annihilation of castes (2)Administration and Finance of the East India Company', (3) 'Evolution of Provincial Finance in British India', (4) 'The Problem of Rupee' (5) 'Small holdings in India and their remedies' and (6) States and Minorities.

From the 1st Five Year Plan onwards various developmental measures were initiated in addition to general developmental programmes for the social and economic development of Dalits (SC/ST). In this context, in the light of Dr. Ambedkar's perspective of economic development of India, an attempt is also made to study the change in the socio-economic status of Dalits (SCs/STs) in terms of their access to land, per capita consumption levels and decline in the incidence of poverty, educational development and change in employment at national level and across the states and human rights. There has been significant improvement in the literacy rates of SCs, STs and the general population in the post-Independence period. However, there is a significant gap between the literacy rate of SCs/STs and the general population in 2011.

Dalits, particularly SCs, mostly remained as agricultural labourers heavily depending on agriculture for their livelihood even after 70 years of Independence without any land base. In states such as Bihar and Andhra Pradesh SC agricultural labour constitutes as much as 69.36% and 64.36% of the total SC workforce, respectively, in 2011. The incidence of poverty is found to be higher among Dalits than among other groups. There has been an increasing per capita consumer expenditure of all social groups in rural areas at the all-India level during the period 1987–1988 to 2009–2010. However, there is a significant gap between the per capita consumer expenditure of SC/STs and others. One important reason for the high incidence of poverty among Dalits, particularly SCs, is the high incidence of landlessness and their heavy dependence on agriculture as agricultural labourers. This is due to the failure of the land reform in Indian agriculture in reducing inequalities in the distribution of land. Hence special measures, like the strict implementation of land reforms, redistributing surplus land, waste lands among Dalits, agricultural labourers and marginal farmers required to be taken up on priority while implementing the programmes, which improve their economic asset base and skills, particularly education as this allows them to shift to non-farming employment.

The book is useful for scholars who work in the areas of Dr. Ambedkar's economic thought and developmental issues of Dalits, in particular, and for all those who are interested to know Dr. Ambedkar's perspective of economic development of India and the developmental issues of Dalits in general.

Gummadi Nancharaiah
Emeritus Professor
School of Economics
University of Hyderabad
Hyderabad

Acknowledgements

This book is the modified version of the report on "Economic Policy and Development of Dalits: Post Independence Period", submitted to ICSSR in June 2018 as an ICSSR National Fellow. I express my gratitude to ICSSR for awarding me the Dr. B. R. Ambedkar National Fellowship (for Studies in Social Justice) for two years, from December 2015 to December 2017.

I am thankful to the University of Hyderabad and Prof. R. Radhakrishna, Chairman, CESS, Hyderabad for nominating my name for the ICSSR National Fellowship.

I am also thankful to my publishers, Routledge, for accepting my work for publication.

I am thankful to the University of Hyderabad administration, the Dean, and the School of Economics for providing me with the office space and necessary infrastructure to work on this project. I also express my thanks to my faculty colleagues for their co-operation.

My special thanks are to Dr. G. Sridevi, Associate Professor, who helped me to carry out the necessary corrections in the manuscript.

I am particularly thankful to Dr. G. Jagadeesh, Research Associate, who assisted me in compiling the required secondary data and typing up the chapters. I am also thankful to the office staff of the School of Economics for their co-operation and their necessary assistance in ensuring that this project work was carried out smoothly. I also thank Matta Srinivas and Patturi Balaji for their assistance in typing and processing the data.

I am thankful to my younger son, Vijay Gummadi, for his valuable comments on the manuscript.

I am thankful to my wife, Mrs. Gummadi Dhanalaxmi, my younger daughter, Srividya Gummadi, and my elder son, Sanjay Gummadi, for their support and co-operation.

I am also thankful to my granddaughter, Samhita Dandangi, for helping me in the design of the cover page for the Asia version of this book.

Gummadi Nancharaiah

1 Dr. Ambedkar's perspective of economic development and its relevance for contemporary India

1.1 Introduction

Ambedkar believed that the state has a crucial role to play in restructuring the society under democratic polity and that the foundations of democracy would be feeble and shaky if there is no social and economic democracy consistent with political democracy. Dr. Ambedkar opined that the existing social and economic institutions, particularly the caste and land tenure system in India, were not conducive to the acceleration of economic development with social justice. Accordingly, he emphasised the need for removing the social and economic inequalities as a precondition for stable democracy and rapid economic development with justice.

After the attainment of Independence right from the 1st Five Year Plan, India adopted a national economic policy with the primary objective of achieving growth with justice. Self-reliance was one of the most important objectives of planning, in addition to the expansion of employment and the removal of poverty. India, like other developing countries, has given priority to import substitution as an effective means of industrialisation. The state was expected to steer the engine of growth and the public sector was assigned a crucial role in the process of industrial development. All of the country's basic and heavy industries were supposed to be brought under the control of the public sector. The emphasis was more on aid than on exports. By the mid-1960s onwards, however, the problem of foreign exchange became very acute due to drought and the war with Pakistan. The policy has been changed to export promotion while continuing import substitution which has been synonymously viewed as self-reliance. Subsequently, several measures to boost exports had been initiated by the Government of India in the form of subsidies to exports and the rupee was devalued by about 57.5% in June 1966 (Sen, 1966, p. 132). Despite the various incentives given to exporting industries and protection for the import-competing industries in the form of tariffs and other controls on imports during the period 1961–1991, there was a negative trade gap which constituted about 3% of GDP on average. The balance of payments problem became very serious in 1991, in part as a result of the fallout from the Gulf War, which was later described as the 1991 economic crisis. Since this time, the

DOI: 10.4324/9781003147053-1

economic policy of India has been liberalised, with an increased emphasis on privatisation and globalisation.

In the post-liberalisation period, particularly during the1990s, although there was some improvement in terms of foreign exchange reserves and the inflow of foreign investment there was no significant improvement in terms of the incidence of poverty and the balance of trade position. Moreover during the 1990s there was a decline in the growth rate of real wages of semi-skilled and unskilled workers. The employment and food production growth rates were much lower in 1990s than they had been in the1980s (Govt. of India, 2001–2002, p. 15). In this context, the views of Dr. Ambedkar on various aspects of Indian economy merit serious discussion.

This chapter attempts to analyse Ambedkar's views on caste and its economic implications, monetary and fiscal systems, exchange rate and trade, Indian agriculture and his plan of economic development and examines their relevance for contemporary India. The required information is drawn from various volumes of *Dr. Babasaheb Ambedkar, writings and speeches* published by the Government of Maharashtra.

1.2 Caste and its economic implications

Ambedkar argued that the caste system as a system of economic organisation did not result in efficiency (Govt of Maharashtra, 1979, Vol. 1, pp. 50–58). It does not represent division of labour on the following grounds.

Caste is not merely division of labour. It is also a division of labourers. It is hierarchical in nature and the division of labourers are graded one above the other. Civilised society undoubtedly requires the division of labour. But in no civilised society the division of labour is accompanied by this unnatural division of labourers into water-tight compartments. In no other country the division of labour is accompanied by the gradation of labourers.

The division of labour represented by the caste system is not spontaneous. It is not based on natural aptitudes. Social and individual efficiency requires the development of the capacity of an individual to the point of competency to choose and make his own career. This is violated in the caste system to the extent that it involves an attempt to assign tasks to individuals in advance not on the basis of trained original capacities, but on the basis of social status of the parents. This is positively pernicious from the point of view of economic development, which is a dynamic phenomenon. Industry is never static; it undergoes rapid changes. Individuals must be free to choose their occupations in a manner compatible with such change. Otherwise, it becomes very difficult for them to make a living. If a Hindu is seen starving rather than taking to new occupation not assigned to his caste, the reason is to be found in the caste. Thus, by not permitting any readjustment of occupations, caste becomes a direct cause of much of the unemployment which exists in the country.

The caste system as a form of division of labour suffers from another serious defect as it is based on the dogma of predestination, in which individual preference plays no role. And certain occupations assigned by the caste system are degraded and the people engaged in such occupations were treated as a defiling group and were given the social stigma of untouchability. As a result, the people engaged in such occupations were provoked to aversion and there was a constant desire to either avoid or escape from such occupations. In a system under which neither men's hearts nor their minds are at work there cannot be any efficiency. As an economic organisation caste is, therefore, a harmful institution in as much as it involves the subordination of man's natural powers and inclinations to the exigencies of social rules (Govt. of Maharashtra, 1979, Vol. 1, p. 48).

Untouchability, which was the by-product of the caste system, was not only a form of social discrimination but also a source of economic exploitation. Untouchables were made to live on the outskirts of the village and physically segregated from the mainstream of society (Govt. of Maharashtra, 1989a, Vol. 5, p. 21). They were assigned those occupations which were unclean and filthy and forced to remain in the same occupations. The untouchables were denied any right to education. They were denied the right of owning land and the right to wage bargaining. They had to perform a number of duties in villages without any remuneration (Govt. of Maharashtra, 1989a, Vol. 5, p. 21). Ambedkar observed that untouchability was more than a religious system. It was also an economic system which was worse than slavery. Untouchability as an economic system permits exploitation without obligation. Untouchability is not only a system of unmitigated economic exploitation but is also a system of uncontrolled economic exploitation (Govt. of Maharashtra, 1989a, Vol. 5, p. 61–87).

In view of the above, Ambedkar argued that there was a need to eliminate the caste system so that there was no contradiction between socio-economic conditions, which existed in the Indian society, and political democracy. Ambedkar, in his speech delivered to the Constituent Assembly on November 25, 1949, referred to contradiction, that is, equality in politics and inequality in social and economic life, the country was going to enter upon after the inauguration of the new constitution on January 26, 1950:

> How long should we continue to live this life of contradiction? How long shall we continue to deny equality in our social and economic life? If we continue to deny for long, we will do so only by putting our political democracy in peril. We must remove this contradiction at the earliest possible moment or else those who suffer from inequality will blow up the structure of political democracy which this assembly has so laboriously built up.

1.3 Dr. Ambedkar's views on the fiscal and monetary system in colonial India and their contemporary relevance

The required information is drawn from the various works of Dr. Ambedkar, including: (1) 'Administration and Finance of the East India Company', (2) 'Evolution of Provincial Finance in British India' and (3) 'The Problem of Rupee'.

Ambedkar dealt with the finances of the East India Company in his work 'Administration and Finance of the East India Company'. Following the proposition of Adam Smith, who asserted that the finances of a country are to be judged from the viewpoint of developmental expenditure, Ambedkar condemned the entire fiscal system of the East India Company. He quotes Mr. Martin who says,

> As the territorial acquisitions of the company expanded the revenue increased with more than commensurate increase of expenditure. The cost of government by Europeans, the growth of standing army in each province and other sources of legitimate or illegitimate expenses swallowing up all the anticipated surplus and leaving nothing for the development of the resources of the country or even for the maintenance of the roads, canals and other public works constructed by native rulers.
>
> (Govt. of Maharashtra, 1989b, Vol. 6, pp. 31–32)

From his analysis of the data on gross revenue and gross expenditure during the period 1792–1793 to 1857–1858, Ambedkar inferred that during this period there were 32 years of surpluses and 14 years of deficit; over the course of this 46-year period there was a surplus of £32 million. But this money was neither saved nor devoted to the works of irrigation or other works of improvement in India. It flowed to England as a continuous payment of dividends to the Company's shareholders and as the flow of money from India proved insufficient to pay the dividends, there was an increasing debt, which was classified as India's public debt. This debt, at least under the period of company rule, was entirely the creation of war. The entire heavy load of the debt of the East India Company, amounting to £694,734,84, was placed on the shoulders of the poverty-stricken natives who had no voice in the doings of the Company. Ambedkar said that this large size of the debt was the result of mismanagement and extravagance on the part of the East India Company and it was one of the important reasons why the discussions about the direct assumption of the Government of India by the Crown even before the mutiny of 1857 took place (ibid., p. 37).

Dr. Ambedkar, in his work 'Evolution of the Provincial Finance in British India', examined the fiscal policy adopted by the Government of India and the financial relationship between the Imperial and Provincial Governments during the period 1833–1919. The imperial system of government was necessarily accompanied by the imperial system of finance from 1833. Dr. Ambedkar observed that the imperial system of government suffered from the financial inadequacy and chronic deficits from 1834–1835 to 1857–1858 and it was only occasionally that finance ministers were successful in restoring equilibrium and avoiding the hour of crisis. He ascribed it to an unsound fiscal policy. The test of sound finance does not consist merely in being capable of raising the requisite amount of revenue as the mode of raising revenue had tremendous implications for the stability and productivity of the economy:

> It is too obvious to be denied that a tax system by its unequal incidence may cause social upheavals just as by its unwise incidence on trade and industry, it may impoverish society by setting out of gear its economic mechanism and technique and eventually beggar the state by impairing the productive powers of the society. The wealth of society is the only patrimony on which the state can draw, and the state that damages it, cannot but end in damaging itself.
>
> (ibid., p. 73)

He also further said that the system of imperial finance established in India was an example of just such a system.

Land tax was one of the important taxes under the imperial system. On the basis of the theory that from time immemorial land was regarded as the property of the state and that the cultivator was not the proprietor but only the occupier, the land tax had been imposed irrespective of the question of necessity or justice. The enhancement of land tax in India has also been justified on the basis of the theory of physiocracy. Dr. Ambedkar observed that heavy rates of taxation on any species of industry, which absorb the whole or nearly the whole of its profits, is ruinous and impolitic. He calculated the ratio of land revenue to the total revenues of India for the period 1792–1793 to 1841–1842 and came to the conclusion that land tax applied at this time was so heavy that the system of tax prevailing in India might well have been called a near approach to the single tax system (ibid., p. 74).

He also opined that while land tax prevented the prosperity of the agricultural industry, customs taxes hampered the manufactures of the country. There were both internal customs and external customs, each of which was injurious to trade and industry. The internal customs were made up of transit and town duties. The country was divided into a number of small customs areas for the purpose of transit duties. Commodities which crossed the customs areas were liable to duty. The transit duties hampered trade which, in turn, crippled the growth of manufacturing industry. The town duties which formed a part of internal customs duties worked towards de-urbanisation (ibid, pp. 75–76).

Under those depressed conditions Indian industry was called upon to meet external competition. But the external duties could not be said to have given any protection to the country, because tariffs were based on political rather than economic considerations. The Indian import tariff was varied not with the nature of the imports, but according to the origin of the imports. Goods from England and goods shipped on English bottoms were charged at half the rate of what good of foreign origin shipped on foreign bottoms was charged. Moreover British goods were allowed into India at lower rates than what the Indian goods had to pay under the internal customs and this was done when England was prohibiting, through the imposition of high tariffs, the entry of Indian-made goods and India-built ships. Indian industry also suffered from heavy export duties. Thus, the custom laws, internal and external, blockaded trade and hampered industry (ibid., p. 77).

Ambedkar also commented that justice in taxation under the imperial regime was conspicuous by its absence:

> The land lords who passed their lives in conspicuous consumption and vicarious leisure on the earnings of the poor tenants, or the many European civil servants who fattened themselves on pay and pickings, were supremely exempted from any contribution towards, the maintenance of the government, whose main activities were directed towards the maintenance of pomp and privilege. On the other hand, the salt tax and the moturpha'[1] and other oppressive taxes continued to harass the industrious poor.Because of this injurious revenue system the taxpaying capacity of the people decayed and as a result the imperial Government was unable to make both ends meet.
>
> (ibid., p. 78)

This tax system, which was based on a unit of land taxes, meant that the poor man who had one acre of land and the landlord who owned hundreds of acres, without realizing the vast income disparities which existed between them, were paying at a uniform rate, which produced a glaring inequity of treatment between rich and poor. Similarly, the salt tax was an example of an oppressive tax system. The pernicious character of the salt tax was urged as a sufficient ground for its elimination from the revenue system of India. But the government not only refused to accept the demand; it actually increased the salt tax rate in 1887–1888 budget to meet the increased deficit while the income tax of 1886 left untouched the incomes of the Bengal Jamindars and the Assam tea planters and the Talukadars of oudh (ibid., p. 230).

Ambedkar further also examined how the revenues raised through such injurious taxes were expended. He found that during the period 1809–1857, military expenditure accounted for more than half of the total revenues and it represented a dead weight on the scanty resources of India. It did not benefit the population, which had contributed to the revenue of the state, from the point of either public utility or private employment. The scales of salaries of European and natives were so grossly unequal that on average a European drew more salary than the salaries of four natives put together.

He also observed that education formed no part of the expenditure incurred and that there relatively few useful public works (ibid., p. 83). Dr. Ambedkar concluded that the collapse of imperial system was due to a faulty fiscal system marked by injurious taxes and unproductive and extravagant expenditure (ibid., p. 88).

1.4 Dr. Ambedkar's view on exchange rate and trade

The view of Dr. Ambedkar on exchange rate[2] and trade can be understood from his work on the problem of the rupee. Dr. Ambedkar analyzed the relationship between exchange rate and external trade in his book,

'The Problem of Rupee'. According to theory, the par of exchange between any two countries will be stable if they employ the same metal functioning as their standard money. On the other hand, there cannot be fixed par of exchange between two countries having different metals as their currency standards. In that case their exchange is governed by the relative values of gold and silver and fluctuates as their relative values change. The gold–silver exchange, which was stable before 1873 between England and India, fluctuated widely after that date. Sterling–rupee exchange, which was a reflection of gold–silver exchange, was also fluctuating after 1873. One reason was the demonetisation of silver as a standard money medium by the principal countries of the world due to the agitation for uniformity of weights, measures and coinages and another was the great increase in the production of silver compared to gold (ibid., pp. 397–403). There was a continuous fall in the exchange rate due to the decline in the relative value of silver in terms of gold and it increased the burden of those which had the obligation to pay in terms of gold. Amongst such, Ambedkar said, the most heavily charged was the Government of India, as it had the obligation to make certain payments to England in terms of gold. But silver being sole legal tender money, the revenues of India were in silver (ibid., p. 416).

The burden of these gold payments increased due to growth in their magnitude and also due to fall in the exchange rate during the period 1875–1892. The excess amount required due to fall in the exchange rate rose from Rs. 411,372,3 to Rs. 654,529,99. The Government of India enforced a policy of high taxes and rigid economy to meet this increased burden. The rates of duty on imported spirits and the excise duties on spirits were not only raised in 1890 but afterwards added to in every province (ibid., p.417). The yield of the taxes and duties levied increased from Rs. 107,230,000 in 1882–1883 to Rs. 161,820,000 in 1892–1893. This entire additional burden was due to the enhanced cost of meeting the gold payments due to the fall in the exchange rate (ibid., p. 417). Despite these measures, the Indian government was in financial difficulties throughout the period of falling exchange rates and could not find any money to undertake public works. The government also inaugurated a policy of 'extra-ordinary public works' financed by the public. Such finance could not be offered by the Indian public, who were poor and often had no savings. India resorted to external borrowings. But foreigners were also reluctant to invest in the rupee securities due to a fall in the value of silver in terms of gold (ibid., p. 419).

But the fall in the exchange rate had a different impact on the trade and industry and it was flourishing compared with the affairs of the Government of India. The level of exports increased from Rs. 575,569,51 in 1870–1871 to Rs. 111,460,278 in 1891–1892 and imports rose from Rs. 399,139,42 to Rs. 841,550,45 during the same period. Not only was the level of trade increasing, but the nature of trade was also changing. India, which was a primary exporting country before 1870, also began to export manufactures. There was a 43% increase in the exports of manufactures during 1879–1892, with the jute and cotton industries showing rapid advances.

After 1870, farming also tended to be more and more market-oriented. During the same period, England, which was on the gold standard, tended to be at a standstill (ibid., pp. 426–430).

There was also a common notion that the bounty arising from the export trade due to the fall in the exchange rate benefited the entire nation. But Ambedkar observed that the bounty was felt because the prices of all goods and services in India did not move uniformly in the same direction. General prices during the period 1873–1893 had fallen in England, but wages had not fallen to the same extent. Prices had risen in India, but wages had not risen to the same extent (ibid., p. 437). The Indian producer received a bounty from this because he did not have to pay higher wages, although the price of his product had risen. The falling exchange rate might have acted as a motivating force to increase exports. But it did so by bringing about changes in the distribution of wealth in the society. In the case of India, where prices were increasing, it was the wage earner who suffered. The fall in the exchange rate, in so far as it was a gain, registered a loss to a large section of the Indian people with fixed incomes (ibid., p. 439).

> Now the class that suffers is the poor labour class which pays the bounty to the richer or the business class. Such transference of wealth from the poor to the rich can never be in the general interest of the country. I therefore strongly oppose the higher prices and low exchange, and righteous government should not be party to such a clandestine picking of the pockets of the poor class in the country.
>
> (ibid., pp. 632–633)

Ambedkar explained domestic prices in terms of the excess creation of currency under the gold exchange standard. From the point of view of economic stability he preferred the gold standard to the gold exchange standard as the discretion of the currency issue was not regulated under the gold exchange standard. The progress of trade depends on the stability of exchange. To maintain exchange rate stability Ambedkar suggested that since all important countries in the world moved towards the gold standard, the silver standard countries should abandon it and move in favour of gold or the gold and silver standard countries have to establish fixed ratio of exchange so as to make the two metals into a common standard of value (ibid., p. 445).

From the above analysis the following can be inferred. The important reasons for the fall of the East India Company and imperial system were government extravagance, unproductive expenditure, public debt and injurious tax system. Due to extravagance, the East India Company was unable to spend money on developmental works. The fiscal policy of government would be sound when the tax policy is not only elastic but also just. And government must control its unproductive expenditure while expending more on progressive works such as roads, irrigation, education and so on. There was also much scope to raise the revenues of government by introducing agricultural income tax instead of a land tax, which was based on a unit of land at a uniform rate. Indirect taxes, particularly salt tax, whose demand is very inelastic, should be completely exempted from state revenue.

It also follows from the above analysis that, according to Ambedkar, a fall in the exchange rate, that is, currency depreciation, leads to an increase in prices thereby causing the redistribution of income in favour of the business class at the cost of the working class, whose wages will not rise in proportion to price raise. As the growth of trade and industry depends on economic stability, there is a strong need to control exchange rate fluctuations within limits. He preferred the gold standard to the gold exchange standard from the point of economic stability and growth with Justice.

1.5 Relevance

When we compare the 1991 economic crisis and subsequent policy changes in fiscal and monetary management in India, we find some similarities and differences between fiscal and monetary problems analysed by Dr. Ambedkar, particularly during the period 1833–1919.

In 1991 there was also an economic crisis which arose because of a huge trade gap, a rising exchange rate, increased prices and an alarming level of external debt. To overcome this, the Government of India initiated a devaluation of the rupee by about 22% in terms of dollar and sterling. Though there was a need to correct the exchange rate by taking into consideration the relative purchasing power of currencies, devaluation cannot solve the problem permanently as, in Ambedkar's view, it causes inflation. After 1991, the Government of India liberalised to a large extent duties on imports; as a result, the negative trade gap was about Rs.31467 crores in 2001–2002 (EPW, 2003, p. 6). It is to be noted here that when there was an increased payments burden during the period 1869–1889, the government of Colonial India raised the level of import duties. Under the new economic policy, the levels of public expenditure on infrastructure, education and other development activities were also reduced, particularly in the early 1990s. But Ambedkar suggested increased expenditure on these items while reducing unproductive expenditure. Ambedkar believed that trade and industry should be encouraged with price stability, but not through exchange rate instability. Foreign investment would not flow unless there was both exchange rate and price stability. The Government of India can mobilise necessary revenues to solve the problem of deficit finance through agricultural income tax, as suggested by Dr. Ambedkar.

1.6 Dr. Ambedkar's views on Indian agricultural development

Indian agriculture has been characterised by a large number of scattered, marginal and small holdings. According to the 2010–2011 agricultural censuses 85.01% of the operational holdings are marginal and small holdings account for 44.58% of the total area under cultivation. Marginal holdings alone constitute 67% of total operational holdings, but control only 22.5% of the total operated area while the top 5% of the total holdings account for more than 31.79% of the total area under cultivation (Agriculture Census in India, 2010–2011, p. 6).

There was a good deal of debate on the relation between the size of the holding and productivity in Indian agriculture. This debate was initiated by A. K. Sen (1962) in his paper "An aspect of Indian agriculture". He stated, on the basis of the farm management survey, that by and large productivity per acre decreased with the size of holding (Sen, 1962, p. 243). This debate also continued into the post-Green Revolution period. It was observed by Ch. Hanumantha Rao and some other economists that the earlier identified inverse relationship under traditional technology no longer holds with the adoption of new technology (Hanumantha Rao, 1980, p. 147). However, recently the inverse relationship between farm size and productivity in Indian agriculture has been established by many studies.

In this context it is interesting to note that Dr. Ambedkar, in his paper on "Small Holdings in India and their remedies" (1918), initiated the discussion on the size of the holding and its effects on productivity in Indian agriculture. It examined the various methods of dealing with the problem of small holdings, which were fragmented. He also proposed state ownership of agriculture and collective farming in his book *States and Minorities* (1947) as a soundest remedy for the problems of Indian agriculture and fostering industrialisation.

An attempt is made (I) to analyse the views of Dr. Ambedkar on the relationship between the size of the holding and its effects on productivity in Indian agriculture and (II) to examine the possible implications of Dr. Ambedkar's proposal of state ownership of agriculture and collective farming as a remedy for the problems of Indian agriculture.

1.7 Consolidation

The problem of consolidation raises the two following issues: (1) how to unite such small and scattered holdings as the existing ones; and (2) once consolidated, how to perpetuate them at that size. The subdivision of land involves what is called the fragmentation of land as the heirs, instead of sharing the lands by survey numbers, claim to share in each survey number, thereby causing fragmentation. Though fragmentation does serve the ends of distributive justice it renders farming in India considerably inefficient and it increases the cost of production. To overcome the problems of fragmentation, the process of consolidation is to be strengthened. He examined the proposals made by R.B.C. (Report of the Committee appointed to make proposals on the consolidation of small and scattered holdings in the Baroda State in 1917), Prof. Jevons and Keatinge, then the Director of Agriculture for the Bombay Presidency (Govt. of Maharashtra, 1979, Vol. 1, p. 456). Ambedkar observed that the principles for consolidation advocated by R.B.C. and Prof. Jevons are almost the same and so is their procedure for carrying it out. Keatinge proposed a one-man rule of succession for the preservation of consolidated holdings while R.B.C. proposed the same only when division of land results in uneconomic holdings. In R.B.C. scheme the other disposed heirs get compensation while Keatinge's scheme does not provide any compensation.

1.8 Enlargement

The enlargement of holdings is as important as their consolidation and it is also desirable that holdings should be economic holdings. But it is believed that a large holding is somehow amore economic holding. In the words of Jevons, an Economic holding is one which produces enough for a farmer to sustain a higher standard of living. According to R.B.C., an Economic holding must be of such a size as having regard to the local conditions of soil, village, etc., necessary to keep one family fully engaged and supported. According to Keatinge, an Economic holding is a holding which allows a man chance of producing sufficient to support himself and his family in reasonable comfort, after paying his necessary expenses (Govt. of Maharashtra, 1979, Vol. 1, p. 466).

Dr. Ambedkar critically examined the above definitions of 'Economic holding' and argued that these definitions view Economic holdings from the point of consumption rather than production. Consumption is not the correct standard to judge the economic character of a holding. In obedience with social custom, a farmer has to support all workers at his disposal, although some of these may be superfluous. Many of the farm enterprises may be regarded as failures if the farm is unable to support all of his family members, even though some could not be productively used, as per the criterion of consumption standards. A true economic relation can subsist only between the total out-turn and the investments; as long as pays for investments, no farm enterprise would be closed, even if it could not support all family members. It follows that Economic holding is to be viewed in terms of production rather than consumption. Although production is for consumption, but it is for those who help to produce (ibid., p. 466).

An ideal proportion that ought to subsist among the various factors combined, though the ideal will vary with the changes in the proportions. The factor proportions would change depending on the elasticity of substitution. Thus, Ambedkar was of the opinion that if agriculture has to be treated as economic enterprise then, by itself, there could be no such thing as small or large. To a farmer a holding may be small or large depending upon the other factors at his disposal. The mere size of the land is empty of all economic connotations and hence it could not be said that a large holding is economic holding while a small holding is uneconomic. It is the right or wrong proportion of other factors of production to a unit of land that renders the latter either economic or uneconomic.

Table 1.1 Change in the agricultural equipment during 1898 to 1910 in Baroda state

Year	*Plough*	*Carts*	*Plough cattle*	*Other domestics*
1898	175,989	–	415,089	570,517
1910	151,664	68,946	334,801	509,416

Source: Govt. of Maharashtra, Dr. Babasaheb Ambedkar Writings and Speeches, Vol. I, 1979, p. 471.

Thus, a small farm may be as economic as a large farm; for economic or uneconomic does not depend upon the size of the land, but upon the due proportions among all the factors, including land (ibid., p. 468). The size of the holding should be allowed to change in response to changes in the equipment which a farmer possesses, to make it economic holding ensuring efficient cultivation and hence size of a holding can be made a large holding but not an economic holding. Therefore, Dr. Ambedkar argues that the proposal of enlarging the existing holdings as a remedy to the ills of Indian agriculture can be entertained only if it is shown that farms have diminished in size while the agricultural stock has increased in amount (ibid., p. 470).

He argued on the basis of some studies (Table 1.1) that there was a deterioration in agricultural equipment during the period 1898–1910.

In light of the above facts, Dr. Ambedkar argues that the existing holdings are uneconomic; not, however, in the sense that they are too small but because they are too large and there is a need for increasing agricultural stock and implements which in turn necessitate enlarged holdings which will be economic holdings as well. Consequently, the remedy for the ills of agriculture in India does not lie primarily in the matter of enlarging holdings, but in the matter of increasing capital and capital goods (Stock of agricultural implements) (ibid., p. 472).

Ambedkar strongly believes that the evils of smallholdings in India are not fundamental, but they are derived from the parent evil of maladjustment in their social economy. He also explained how we suffered from bad social economy (ibid, p. 472). He showed that a little land was cultivated in proportion to population in India on the basis of the data presented and argued that a large part of the agricultural population is superfluous and idle.

Dr. Ambedkar argued that of the total population of 254 million in 1881, nearly two-thirds were agricultural and as per estimate allowing one-third to be taken up, we can safely say that a population of equal magnitude was lying idle instead of performing any sort of productive labour. With the increasing ruralisation of India and a continually decreasing proportion of land under cultivation, the volume of idle labour must have increased to an enormous extent. He also argued that the increased pressure on land was the chief cause of the subdivision of land.

He did not agree to the view that the law of inheritance causes the subdivision of land. Naturally, population that has little else to prefer to agriculture will try to invoke every possible cause to get a piece of land, however small. It is not therefore the law of inheritance that is the evil, but rather the high pressure on land which brings it into operation. Thus, the universal prevalence of small farms of petit culture is due to this enormous pressure on land (ibid., p. 474).

He draws the distinction between idle labour and idle capital and explains the effects of idle labour. Capital exists but labour lives. That is to say capital, when idle, does not earn, but does not also consume much to keep itself. But labour, earning or not consumes in order to live. Idle labour is therefore a calamity: for if it cannot live by production as it should, it will live by predation as it must. Instead of contributing to our national dividend it is eating up what little there is of it. Thus, the depression of national dividend is another important effect of idle labour. Since a large portion of our society makes little current effort due to the existence of idle labour there can be no surplus and hence no capital, which is nothing but crystallised surplus. Thus, he argued that our bad social economy was responsible for the ills of our agriculture and that our entire dependence on agriculture leads to small and scattered farms and the existence of idle labour makes ours a county without capital (ibid., p. 475).

He further explained how the remedies suggested above for consolidation and enlargement under the existing social economy are bound to fail. They will inevitably lead to an increase in the army of landless and disposed men, which is neither cheerful from the individual point of view nor agreeable from the national point of view. If the agricultural system is made capitalist, it aggravates the evils by adding to our stock of idle labour, for capitalist agriculture will not need as many hands as are now required by our present day methods of cultivation.

According to Ambedkar, the remedy is to shift this labour to non-agricultural channels of production where it can be used productively. When it is thus employed, it ceases to live by predation as it does today and will not only earn to keep itself, but will give us surplus and more surplus is more capital. This means that the industrialisation of India is the soundest remedy for the agricultural problems of India (ibid., p. 477).

Industrialisation reduces pressure on agriculture and increases the amount of capital goods which will forcibly create the economic necessity of enlarging the holding. By legislation, we will get some economic holding at the cost of many social ills. But by industrialisation a large economic holding will force itself upon us a pure gain. While he was sure of industrialisation as an effective remedy for enlargement and it will be the most effective barrier against sub-division and fragmentation, he realised that industrialisation will not be a sufficient remedy for consolidation. But it will facilitate consolidation by lessening the premium on land. "Thus if small and scattered holdings are the ills from which our agriculture is suffering to cure it of them is undeniably to industrialize" (ibid. p. 479).

1.9 Conclusion

From the above analysis it follows that the efficient production requires the ideal combination of all other factors of production to a unit of land. It is the right or wrong proportion of factors of production to unit of land that renders the latter as economic or uneconomic. The mere size of land holding is empty of all economic connotations and hence it could not be said that a large holding is economic while a small holding is uneconomic. As there is a change in the amount of farm equipment a farmer owns, the size of the farm should also be allowed to change, to make it an economic holding and thereby ensure efficient production.

Under the existing conditions of social economy, Dr. Ambedkar observed, the proposed remedies of either one-man rule of succession or expansion of capital for enlarging and consolidating are bound to fail as they would add to the existing levels of idle labour. Therefore, the remedy is to shift the idle labour to the non-agricultural channels of production. This means the industrialisation of India is the soundest remedy for agricultural problems in India. Industrialisation, while reducing the pressure on land, increases the amount of capital which will in turn create large economic holdings and foster industrial development. However, Ambedkar proposed the collectivisation of agriculture in 1947 in order to solve the problems of Indian Agriculture.

1.10 Dr. Ambedkar's plan of economic development

Dr. Ambedkar presented his plan of economic development in his book *States &Minorities* (1947), in which he emphasised the introduction of state socialism in important aspects of economic life. The state socialism proposed by Dr. B.R. Ambedkar has the following salient features (Govt. of Maharashtra, 1979, Vol. 1, pp. 411–412):

1. Industries which are key industries or which may be declared to be key industries shall be owned and run by the state.
2. The Industries which are not key industries but which are basic industries shall be owned by the state and shall be run by the state or by corporation established by the state.
3. The insurance shall be the monopoly of the state and that the state shall compel every adult citizen to take out a life insurance policy commensurate with his wages as may be prescribed by the legislature.
4. The agricultural industry shall be state industry.
5. The state shall acquire the subsisting rights in such industries, insurance and agricultural land held by private individuals, whether as owners, tenants or mortgages and pay them compensation in the form of debenture equal to the value of his or her right in the land.
6. The state shall also determine how and when the debenture holder shall be entitled to claim cash payment.

7. The debenture shall be transferable and inheritable property but neither the debenture holder nor the transferee from the original holder nor his heir shall be entitled to claim the return of the land nor enters in any industrial concern acquired by the state nor be entitled to deal with it in any way.
8. The debenture-holder shall be entitled to interest on his debenture as such rate as may be defined by law, to be paid by the state in cash or in kind as the state may deem it fit.
9. Agricultural industry shall be organised on the following basis-
   (i) The state shall divide the land acquired into farms of standard size and let out the farm for cultivation to residents of the village as tenants (made up of group of families) to cultivate on the following conditions:-
      a. The farm shall be cultivated as a collective farm
      b. The farm shall be cultivated in accordance with rules and directions issued by government.
      c. The tenants shall share among themselves, in the manner prescribed, the produce of the farm left after the payment of the charges properly levyable on the farm.
   (ii) The land shall be let out to villagers without distinction of caste or creed and in such manner that there will be no landlord, no tenant and no landless labour.
   (iii) It shall be the obligation of the state to finance the cultivation of the collective farms by the supply of water, drought animals, implements, manure, seeds etc.
   (iv) The state shall be entitled to
      a. Levy the following charges on the produce of the farm:
         a.1 a portion for land revenue
         a.2 a portion to pay debenture holders, and
         a.3 a portion to pay for the use of capital goods supplied, and
      b. to prescribe penalties against the tenants who break the conditions of tenancy or willfully neglect to make the best use of the means of cultivation offered by the state or otherwise act prejudicially to the scheme of collective farming.
10. The scheme shall be brought into operation as early as possible but in no case shall the period extend beyond the tenth year from the date of the constitution coming into operation.

Thus he proposed state ownership of agriculture with a collectivised method of cultivation and modified form of state socialism in the field Industry.

Dr. Ambedkar also proposed that the above scheme of state socialism should not be left to the will of the legislature; rather, it should be established by the law of constitution so that it will be beyond the reach of a parliamentary majority to suspend, amend or abrogate it. This guarantees state socialism while retaining parliamentary democracy. "It is only by this that one can achieve the triple objects namely, establish socialism, retain parliamentary democracy and avoid dictatorship". Dr. Ambedkar also believed that his plan of state socialism was essential for rapid industrialisation, increasing productivity without closing every avenue to private sector and also for distributing wealth equitably.

> The main purpose behind this clause is to put an obligation on the state to plan the economic life of the people on lines which would lead to the highest point of productivity without closing every avenue to the private enterprise and also provide for the equitable distribution of wealth.
>
> (ibid., p. 408)

Further Dr. Ambedkar also argued that if democracy was to live up to its principle of "one man one value", it was essential to define both the economic structure as well as the political structure of society by the Law of Constitution.

1.11 The relevance of collective farming

It is true that to solve the problems of agriculture collective farms under state control had been adopted in the USSR. This gave security of employment and minimum income to agricultural labourers in addition to solving the problems of inequality in the distribution of wealth and income. Through this system, the basic problem of rural poverty was solved. The congress agrarian reforms committee, under the chairmanship of J.C Kumarappa (1940), rejected the concept of capitalist farming as the form of agricultural organisation on the ground that it would deprive the agriculturists of their rights in land and turn them into mere wage earners. It would also create the problem of the disposed personnel. It was held that peasant farming would be the most appropriate form of cultivation above the basic holding, but that the smaller holding should be brought under the scheme of cooperative farming. It was also held that the collective farming would be more suitable for the development of reclaimed waste lands on which landless labourers could be settled (Haque and Sirohi 1986, p. 100). This was also supported further by the debate on farm size and productivity, initiated by A.K. Sen, who writes that "for example if a large cooperative farm operates on a non-wage family labour basis, there is nothing in our observation to indicate that it will have to lower output per acre..." (Sen, 1962, p. 246). However, cooperative farming did not materialise, although family-based peasant farming was adopted in India. Land reforms could abolish intermediaries, but land concentration persists and it is the most important reason for the existence of a higher incidence of rural poverty despite tremendous increases in food production as a result of the Green Revolution.

In India, a large proportion of the agricultural labouring population come from depressed sections which suffer from social discrimination and economic exploitation. The condition of agricultural labourers was worse, particularly on the eve of Independence, and collectivisation would have definitely solved their basic problems of poverty had we opted for the collectivisation of farms. However, collective farming under state control was subjected to much criticism after the collapse of communism in Eastern Europe, particularly in the USSR, and a subsequent shift to market-oriented strategies of development. It was pointed out that when minimum needs were met by the state in a regime of collective farming, the state used to take decisions regarding what to produce and how to produce, irrespective of cost considerations, without involving farmers in decision-making. This was one of the reasons for the failure of state farming. It is true that agriculture requires a level of personal attention which is lacking in collective farming. This implies that productivity suffers due to the lack of personal attention and the incentive to increase production. This means that collective farming under the state helps in solving basic problems of poverty initially, but it may not lead to increased productivity. Personal attention and incentives to produce more is ensured in the case of family-based peasant farming above basic limit. But collective farming is better suited in the case of marginal farms, which constitute 60% of agricultural holdings, but control only about 20% of area under cultivation in India. Furthermore, the state should take the responsibility of supplying necessary capital and other inputs.

Thus, it follows from the above analysis of D.R. Ambedkar's perspective of development that the state has to play a very active and crucial role in accelerating the achievement of growth with Justice through democratic methods. The foundation of democracy would be feeble and shaky if the contradictions between political democracy, enshrined in the constitution, and social and economic inequalities, which exist in our society, are not resolved.

When we examine the role of the state in some of the East Asian Countries such as South Korea and Taiwan (Province of China), which have registered significant growth rates, we understand that the state has played a very important role while opening the economy to market forces.

In South Korea in the period after liberation, there were two important institutional changes in agriculture and industry which had significant long-term implications for the country's economic development. Land reform was initiated in 1948. It set a limit of three hectares on the ownership and virtually abolished tenancy. The landlord's holdings were virtually confiscated and redistributed. This reform reduced social and political tensions in the countryside. It also led to an increase in agricultural production and a more even distribution of income and wealth. Educational reforms laid an emphasis on improving primary, secondary and technical education. In 1980, the rate of literacy in the labour force was 100%. Educational reforms laid the foundation for the creation of an educated and skilled labour force, which was essential for the success of any industrial policy (E Prime Eshang, EPW, 1991, pp. 629–643).

Thus, the success of South Korea, with its outward-looking strategy, is the result of state intervention which could bring necessary internal reform and regulate markets. This is also true in the case of Taiwan (Province of China), where land reform also had a very positive impact on employment in Taiwan (Province of China). After the reforms, the number of people involved in agriculture increased rapidly from 400,000 to about two million between 1952 and 1968. There was also a substantial increase in output. In addition to redistributing assets simultaneously, investment was made in health, education and skills of their people. Labour productivity has been increasing at an annual rate of 10% or more, half of which has been attributed to investment in education and technical skills (UNDP, 1993, p. 38).

In the light of the experience of South Korea and Taiwan, it becomes obvious that the state has a crucial and active role to play and that the industrial strategy of development must also be labour-intensive in the case of India. Land reform and educational reform are preconditions, even for the success of economic liberalisation.

Now let us look at the present socio-economic conditions in India. The percentage of people below the poverty line was estimated by the planning commission as 21.9% at the all-India level in 2011–2012 (Govt. of India, 2013, p. 2). About 48.9% of the workforce depends on agriculture and its allied sectors and agriculture contributes to 17.5% of total GDP(Economic Survey, 2015–2016, p. 98). According to the 2011 population census, 68.86% of the total population live in rural areas. As per the 2010–2011 agricultural census, 67% of marginal holdings accounted for about 22.5% of the total area under cultivation while the top 5% of the total holdings account for more than 31.79% of the total area under cultivation (Agriculture Census in India, 2010–2011).The distribution of land remains skewed despite land reforms. This is mostly responsible for the social tensions in rural India. In addition to economic inequalities, Indian society is characterised by social inequalities resulting from the caste system. Moreover, 26.60% of the total population is illiterate as per 2011 census.

Hence, given the current stage and structure of the present-day Indian economy, Dr. Ambedkar's perspective of development, with its emphasis on an active state role in bringing about the desired change in socio-economic institutions to accelerate the policy aim of growth with Justice is relevant.

Notes

1 A tax on trades and occupations embracing weavers, carpenters, all workers in metals, all salesmen whether possessing shops which are taxed separately, or vending by the roadside, etc., some paying imports on their tools, others for permission to sell, extending to the most trifling articles of trade and the cheapest tools machines can employ, the cost of which frequently exceeded six times over by the moturpha under which the use of them is permitted" (*Dr. Ambedkar, Writing and speeches*, Vol. 6, 1989, p. 78).

2 "Exchange rate was defined as number of units of foreign currency to be obtained for one unit of Indian currency. However at present exchange rate is defined as number of units of domestic currency to be paid for one unit of foreign currency.

References

Eprime Eshang. (1991). Successful manipulation of market forces: Case of South Korea, 1961–78. *Economic & Political Weekly*, XXVI(11 and 12), Annual Number 1991.

EPW Research Foundation. (2003). Current statistics. *Economic and Political Weekly*, 38(1), p. 6.

Government of India. (2014). *Agriculture Census in India, 2010–2011, All India Report on Number and Area of Operational Holdings, Agriculture*. Census Division, Department of Agriculture & Co-operation, Ministry of Agriculture, Government of India, New Delhi.

Government of India. (2015–2016). *Economic Survey*, Ministry of Finance, New Delhi.

Government of Maharashtra. (1979). *Dr. Babasaheb Ambedkar Writings& Speeches*, Vol. 1, Edition by Education Department, Govt. of Maharashtra, Bombay.

Government of Maharashtra. (1989a). *Dr. Babasaheb Ambedkar Writings & Speeches*, Vol. 5, Edition by Education Department, Govt. of Maharashtra, Bombay.

Government of Maharashtra. (1989b). *Dr. Babasaheb Ambedkar Writings & Speeches*, Vol. 6, Edition by Education Department, Govt. of Maharashtra, Bombay.

Hanumantha Rao, C.H.(1980). *Technological Changes and Distribution of Gains in Indian Agriculture*. Macmillan & Co., New Delhi.

Haque, T. and Sirohi, A.S. (1986). *Agrarian Reforms and Institutional Change in India*. Concept Publishing Company, New Delhi.

Planning Commission. (2013).*Press Note on Poverty Estimates, 2011–12*. Government of India, New Delhi.

Sen, A.K. (1962). An aspect of Indian agriculture. *Economic Weekly*. 1962; Annual Number 14.

Sen, P. (1966). The 1966 evaluation in India, are-appraisal. *EPW*, XXI(30), July 26, 1986.

United National Development Programme-Human Development Report. (1993). Oxford University Press, Delhi.

2 Dr. Ambedkar on education and educational development of Dalits in India

2.1 Introduction

This chapter attempts to study the position of Dalits and their access to education in colonial India and also the change in their educational status in the post-Independence period. This chapter draws heavily on the publication by the Government of Maharashtra, *Dr. Babasaheb Ambedkar: writings and speeches* (1993), Vol. 12 for an understanding of Dalits' access to education in colonial India. Ambedkar took the Bombay presidency by way of illustration and examined the position and access of Dalits to education during colonial rule. In order to study the change in the educational status of Dalits in the post-Independence period. The chapter makes use of secondary data obtained from 'Educational statistics at a Glance', Government of India, XI Five Year Plan, 2007–2012 Document, Selected Educational Statistics 2005–2006, Population Census, 2011 and Statistics of School Education 2010–2011. This chapter covers literacy rates and dropout rates across different social groups at the national level as well as among the states, and also gross enrolment ratios in primary, secondary and higher education at the national level.

2.2 Dalits' education in colonial India

Under the Peshwas the depressed classes were entirely beyond the pale of education. They found no place in state education for the simple reason that the Peshwas government was a theocracy based upon the canons of Manu, according to which the Shudras and Atishudras (backward classes) had no individual rights to education. The depressed classes, who were labouring under such disabilities, breathed a sigh of relief at the downfall of this hated theocracy (Government of Maharashtra, *Dr. Babasaheb Ambedkar: writings and speeches* (1993), Vol. 12, p. 94).

For a long time the British were silent on the question of promoting education among the native population. In 1813 the British parliament stated: "Out of the surplus revenues of India, a sum of not less than one lakh of rupees in each year shall be set apart and applied to the revival and improvement of literature and the encouragement of the learned natives of

DOI: 10.4324/9781003147053-2

India, and for the introduction and promotion of knowledge of the science among the inhabitants of British territories in India, etc". In 1814 court of directors ruled that the promotion of Sanskrit learning among the Hindus would fulfill the purpose which parliament had in mind. But the depressed classes were totally disappointed, as this meant that education would be a preserve of the higher classes. The honourable court wrote to Madras in 1830 as follows:

> The improvement in education, however, which most effectively contribute to elevate the moral and intellectual conditions of the people, are those which concern the education of the higher classes of the persons possessing leisure and natural influence over the minds of their countrymen. By raising the standard of instructions amongst these classes you would eventually produce a much greater and morally beneficial change in the ideas and feelings of the community than you can hope to produce by acting directly in the more numerous classes.
>
> (ibid., p. 96)

No schools were opened for depressed classes before 1855 in the Bombay Presidency; it was because the deliberate policy of the British Government was to restrict the benefits of higher education to the higher castes, chiefly the Brahmins and other upper classes. The Depressed classes were not allowed by government to have a share in education (ibid., pp. 95–96).

However, from 1854 onwards measures were taken to spread education to the masses of the country. The directives of the court observed, in 1854:

> Our attention should now be directed to a consideration, if possible, still more important, and one which has hitherto, we are bound to admit, been much neglected, namely, how useful and practical knowledge suited to every station in life, may be best conveyed to the great mass of the people who are utterly incapable of obtaining any education worthy of the name by their own efforts; and we desire to see the active measures of Government more especially directed, for the future, to this object, for the attainment of which, we are ready to sanction a considerable increase of expenditure.
>
> (ibid., p. 101)

The results of this policy were first examined by the Hunter Commission on Indian Education, which was published in 1882.The figures in Tables 2.1, 2.2 and 2.3 summarise these results. They show that although the government policy was committed to mass education, the mass were just as excluded from education as they had been before 1854, and that the lowest classes of Hindus still remained lowest in order of education. In 1881–1882, for example, there was no student from that community in either the High Schools or the Colleges of this Presidency. The dismal

Table 2.1 Primary education in Bombay Presidency, 1881–1882

	No. of students at school	*Per cent of total*
Christians	1,521	0.49
Brahmins	63,071	20.17
Other Hindus	202,345	64.69
Mohammedans	39,231	12.54
Parsis	3,517	1.12
Aboriginal and Hill Tribes	2,713	0.87
Low Caste Hindus	2,862	0.87
Jews and Others	373	0.12

Source: Govt. of Maharashtra, *Dr. Babasaheb Ambedkar, writings and speeches*, Vol. 12, 1993, pp. 102–103.

Table 2.2 Secondary education in Bombay Presidency, 1881–1882

	Middle Schools		*High Schools*	
	No. of students	*% of total*	*No. of students*	*% of total*
Christians	1,429	12.06	111	2.26
Brahmins	3,639	30.70	1,978	40.29
Other Hindus	-	-	-	-
Cultivators	624	5.26	140	2.85
Low Castes	17	0.14	-	-
Other Castes	3,823	32.25	1,573	32.04
Mohammedans	687	5.80	100	2.04
Parsis	1,526	12.87	965	19.66
Aboriginal and Hill Tribes	6	0.05	-	-
Others (including Jews)	103	0.87	92	0.86

Source: Govt. of Maharashtra, *Dr. Babasaheb Ambedkar, writings and speeches*, Vol. 12, 1993, pp. 102–103.

Table 2.3 Collegiate education in the Bombay Presidency, 1881–1882

	No. of students	*% of total*
Christians	14	3
Brahmins	241	50
Other Hindus	-	-
Cultivators	5	1
Low Castes	0	0
Other Castes	103	21.3
Mohammedans	7	1.5
Parsis	108	21.5
Aboriginal and Hill Tribes	0	0
Others (including Jews)	2	0.4

Source: Govt. of Maharashtra, *Dr. Babasaheb Ambedkar, writings and speeches*, Vol. 12, 1993, pp. 102–103.

performance of the Dalits in education was because there were some who were agitating for a reversal of the policy of mass education.

The fears of dire consequences for British rule of elevating the lower classes above their standing in life used to haunt men like Lord Ellenborough, President of the Board of Control, who expressed his concerns to the Court of Directors on 28 April 1858.

> Education and civilization may descend from the higher to the inferior classes, and so communicated may impart new vigour to the community, but they will never ascend from the lower classes to those above them; they can only, if imparted solely to the lower classes, lead to general convulsion, of which foreigners would be the first victims. If we desire to diffuse education, let us endeavour to give it to the higher classes first, By founding colleges to which the higher classes alone should be admitted, and by giving in the reorganization of the army, commissions at once, to such sons of native gentlemen as may be competent to receive them.
>
> (ibid., p. 104)

The antipathy of the European officers towards the untouchable classes was corrected by the Secretary of India in 1859. He reiterated the responsibility of the government for mass education schools were opened for the depressed classes. But the question of the admission of the depressed classes to these schools had yet to be resolved. In 1856, for example, when a Mahar boy was denied admission to the Dharwar government school, the decision of the government was unfavourable to the depressed classes. In Bengal, untouchables also had some problems, as caste Hindus declined to sit with them in school. Thus, mass education was available to all except the depressed classes. In an attempt to address the situation, the government supported separate schools for the depressed class and allowed grants to missionary bodies to run them by relaxing the rules for grants-in-aid (ibid., pp. 104–107).

After the year 1882, the year 1923 forms the next landmark in the educational history of the Bombay Presidency. This year marks the transfer of primary education from the control of Provincial Governments to the control of local bodies. Table 2.4 gives the position of the different communities in the matter of educational advancement. The intermediate class, which is the first in terms of population, is third in order of college education, third in order of secondary education and third in order of primary education. The depressed (or backward) classes, who are second in order of population, stand fourth, i.e., last in order of college education, last in order of secondary education and last in order of primary education. The Mahomedans, who are third in order of population, are second in order of college education, second in order of secondary education and second in order of primary education. while the advanced Hindus, who occupy the fourth place in terms of population, stand first in order of college education, first in order of secondary education and first in order of primary education.

Table 2.4 Classes of population in the Bombay Presidency, 1923

	Order in respect of population	*Primary*	*Secondary*	*College*
Advanced Hindus	4th	1st	1st	1st
Intermediate Hindus	1st	3rd	3rd	3rd
Backward Hindus	2nd	4th	4th	4th
Mahomedans	3rd	2nd	2nd	2nd

Source: Govt. of Maharashtra, *Dr. Babasaheb Ambedkar, writings and speeches*, Vol. 12, 1993, p. 108.

Table 2.5 State of education in the Bombay Presidency, 1923

	Primary	*Secondary*	*College*
	Students per 1000 population	*Students per 1000 population*	*Students per 1000 population*
Advanced Hindus	119	3000	1000
Intermediate Hindus	92	500	52
Backward Hindus	38	140	24
Mahomedans	18	14	Approx.0

Source: Govt. of Maharashtra, *Dr. Babasaheb Ambedkar, writings and speeches*, Vol. 12, 1993, p. 109.

Table 2.5 highlights the disparities among the classes. The state of education of the backward classes is seen to be deplorable in this presidency. In terms of population they occupy second place, but in the matter of education they occupy not only the last place but also the least. This is the result of the negligence of the government regarding the provision of the education in the backward classes. The resolution of its Department of Education, dated 21 February 1923, which extended funds to local government, notes the educational needs of the domiciled community and Mohammedans, but there is no word about the depressed class. (ibid, pp. 110–114)

2.3 Dr. Ambedkar's views on education

Ambedkar pleaded in the Bombay legislative council in 1927 that we should at least spend on education the same amount that we take from the people in the form of excise revenue. The amount of expenditure that we incur per individual in this presidency on education is only 14 annas, but the amount of money that we recover in the form of excise revenue is Rs. 2-2-9 (Rs. 2.17) (Govt. of Maharashtra, 1982, Vol. II, pp. 39–40).

He observes that the object of primary education is to ensure that every child who enters the portals of a primary school does leaves it only at a stage when they have become literate and that they continue to be literate throughout their life. If we consider the statistics, however, we find that of every hundred children that enter a primary school only eighteen reach the fourth standard; the rest of them, that is to say, 82 of every 100 relapse into the state of illiteracy. Ambedkar argues that unless we spend sufficient sums of money, to see that every child that enters a school reaches the fourth standard, what we have already spent upon him is of no purpose what so ever (ibid., p. 40).

He also strongly opposes the commercialisation of education:

> Education is something which ought to be brought within the reach of everyone. The Education Department is not a department which can be treated on the basis of *quid pro quo*. Education ought to be cheapened in all possible ways and to the greatest possible extent.
>
> (ibid., pp. 40–41)

He urges this plea because he feels that we are arriving at a stage when the lower orders of society are just getting into the high schools, middle schools and colleges.

He emphasises that this country is composed of different communities and these communities are all unequal in their status and progress. He argues that if they are to be brought to the level of equality, then the only remedy is to adopt the principle of inequality and to give favoured treatment to those who are below this level:

> There are some I know who object to this and adhere to the principle of equality of treatment. But I say Government has done well in applying this principle to the Mahomedans. For I honestly believe that equality of treatment to people who are unequal is simply another name for indifferentism and neglect. My only complaint is that Government has not yet thought fit to apply this principle to the backward classes. Economically speaking or socially speaking, backward classes are handicapped in a manner in which no other community is handicapped. I, therefore, think that the principle of favoured treatment must be adopted in their case.
>
> (ibid., p. 42)

He mentions that the Primary Education Act is a great wrong. In fact, it is doubly wrong. It is wrong because the responsibility of education is transferred to the hands of those who are not enlightened enough to understand that education is a great necessity. If there are any people who realise the necessity for education they are not to be found in this Council. The members of the local boards are too uneducated to realise that education is a necessity. Therefore, he says this Council has done a great wrong in transferring the responsibility for education to the hands of those people who do not feel for education. Again, the transfer of education to local bodies is a wrong because the burden has thereby been transferred to shoulders less broad to bear it. He also says education of the masse, is a matter of great cost and if there is any body which can be said to be able to bear it, it is this Council with its revenue of 15½ crores and not the local bodies with their meagre revenues of a few lakhs (ibid., p. 43).

> I feel, Sir that this Council in transferring education to the local bodies has practically postponed the spread of education among the 'masses' *sine die* and in doing so has gravely erred. But, Sir, this is only preliminary to, the point which I wish to make, namely that the people who are the greatest sufferers by this wrong are the depressed classes.
>
> (ibid., p. 43)

Regarding the method of giving scholarship to the boy of depressed classes Dr. Ambedkar opines that scholarship as an aid is better than no aid at all. However, it would be better if the government spends this money in promoting hostels for the promotion of education of backward classes as it weans the boy from evil surroundings and provides effective control (ibid., p. 44).

2.4 On the Bombay University Act Amendment Bill

Dr. Ambedkar opines that University cannot succeed in promoting research or in promoting higher education, if it makes the examination system the be-all and end all of its existence (ibid., pp. 45–46).

He argues that University should undertake undergraduate teaching. He opines that if the object is to promote higher education and research the best methods would be not to separate the college from the university as has been done now but to make a synthesis in which the university and college would be participating in promoting together, both the undergraduate and post graduate students (ibid., p. 48). University to localise teaching by giving greater control over colleges which may be called "constituent colleges" situated in geographically compact centres (ibid., p. 50). Ambedkar opines that unless the University undertakes undergraduate teaching, any amount of super-imposition of post-graduate work will not be of any avail whatsoever. (ibid., p. 46). University which merely super-imposes postgraduate work upon it cannot succeed in promoting real knowledge or real research (ibid., p. 47).

He makes the case for the representation of backward classes and depressed classes on the senate of the university. No community, however intellectually advanced it may be, can be the guardians of other communities. (ibid., p. 50)

> One thing is that Every access must be given to every grade of modern education to the communities which are educationally backward, in order that they may realise their rights and liabilities of citizenship, and secondly, in order that every access may be given to these communities,

> it is absolutely necessary, under the present circumstances, that special representation should be provided for them.
>
> (ibid., p. 52)

One of the fundamental functions of the University is to provide facilities for bringing the highest education to the doors of the needy and the poor (ibid., p. 61). He also observes

> Backward classes have come to realise that after all education is the greatest material benefit for which they can fight. We may forego material benefits of civilization, but we cannot forego our right and opportunity to reap the benefit of the highest education to the fullest extent. Backward classes who have just realized that without education their existence is not safe.
>
> (ibid., p. 62)

Dr. Ambedkar founded the People's Education Society on 8 July 1945 for the promotion of educational development of the people in general, and in Scheduled Castes and Scheduled Tribes in particular. Under the auspices of the people's education society, he founded the Siddhartha College at Bombay on 20 June 1946. This institution was named after Buddha, as he was a figure who embodied social, intellectual and political freedom. The people's education society also founded the Milind College at Aurangabad and its foundation stone was laid by Dr. Rajendra Prasad in September 1951. King Milind, after whom the institution was named, was one of the country's great Buddhist scholars. Both of these colleges have grown in strength and stature over the years. The people's education society started many more such institutions at various places. These colleges were open to the students of all the castes and creeds. The main criterion for appointment of teachers in these colleges was merit only (Shahare, 1991, pp. 137–138).

2.5 The post-Independence period

After independence, and particularly from the time of the First Five Year Plan onwards, various special developmental measures were initiated in addition to general development programmes for the social and economic development of Dalits. Initially, the state was expected to play an active and crucial role in the process of development. The public sector was expected to control the commanding heights of the economy. This sector not only had the economic objective of maximisation of profits but also providing access to deprived sections in the process of development and whereby reduces the inequalities in the distribution of wealth as the economy develops.

The Scheduled Caste population, which constituted 14.6% of the total population in 1951, had increased to 16.6% of the total population of the country by 2011, while the Scheduled Tribe population, which was 6.2% in 1951 increased to 8.6% of the total population of the country in 2011 (Table 2.6).

Table 2.6 Trends in proportion of Scheduled Caste and Scheduled Tribe population

Census Year	*Total population (in million)*	*Scheduled Castes population (in million)*	*Proportion of SCs population*	*Scheduled Tribes population (in million)*	*Proportion of STs population*
1951	356	52	14.6	-	-
1961	439.2	65	14.7	30	6.9
1971	547.9	80	14.6	38	6.9
1981	665.3	106	15.7	52	7.8
1991	838.6	138	16.5	68	8.1
2001	1028.6	167	16.2	85	8.2
2011	1210.1	201	16.6	104	8.6

Source: *Educational Statistics at a Glance*, Government of India, Ministry of Human Resource Development Bureau of Planning, Monitoring & Statistics, New Delhi, 2014.

2.6 Access to education

In the case of social sectors like education and health special attention has to be paid as these are both important components of human resource development. Education not only improves the skills of people, leading to an increase in the level of productivity but also acts as an agent of social change. Education, particularly technical and vocational education, helps people to securing employment and increase their levels of income and consumption and also alleviates their socio-economic status. Ambedkar viewed education as not only an important instrument of economic development and an agent of social change, but it also equips Dalits to fight for their human rights.

The Government of India has been allocating the 50% welfare outlay meant for the social and economic development of Dalits for educational development since the First Five Year Plan. The details of change in the levels of literacy among different social groups are presented in Table 2.7.

Table 2.7 Literacy rates of SC/ST by sex from 1961 to 2011

	General			*Scheduled Castes*			*Scheduled Tribes*		
Year	*Males*	*Females*	*Persons*	*Males*	*Females*	*Persons*	*Males*	*Females*	*Persons*
1961	34.44	12.95	24.02	17	3.29	10.27	13.83	3.16	8.53
1971	39.45	18.7	29.45	22.4	6.44	14.67	17.63	4.85	11.3
1981	46.89	24.82	36.23	31.1	10.93	21.38	24.52	8.04	16.35
1991	52.74	32.17	42.84	40.24	19.03	30.07	32.5	14.5	23.63
2001	63.24	45.15	54.51	55.1	34.62	45.2	48.23	28.36	38.41
2011	80.9	64.6	73.0	75.2	56.5	66.1	68.5	49.4	59.0

Source: *Educational Statistics at a Glance*, Government of India, Ministry of Human Resource Development Bureau of Planning, Monitoring & Statistics, New Delhi, 2014.

2.7 Literacy rates

It can be seen from the Table 2.7 that the literacy rate of Scheduled Castes increased from 10.27 in 1961 to 66.1 in 2011, while the literacy rates of Scheduled Tribes increased from 8.53% to 59.0% during the same period. It is to be noted from the table that the percentages of literacy rates of SC/ST are always lower when compared with the literacy percentage of general population.

Although the literacy rate of SC/STs has increased considerably over the period from 1961 to 2011, there is still a significant gap between the literacy rate of the other population groups and that of SC/STs. There is a literacy gap of 6.9% between SCs and others and 14.0% between STs and others. The gap is still wide between SC/STs female literacy rates and that of other females in 2012–2013 (Table 2.8).

2.8 Dropout rates

The school dropout rate is a crucial indicator of the lack of educational development. The dropout rates for SC children remain very high: 32.7% in Classes I to V; 55.2% in Classes I to VIII; and 69.1% in classes I to X in 2004–2005. The gap between the SC population and the general category increases at higher levels of schooling, Although dropout rates have fallen in 2012–2013. They are found to be on the higher side in case of class 1-Xwith reference to SC/STs (Table 2.9).

Table 2.8 Literacy gap of SC/ST to others in 2011

	Literacy rates			*Literacy gap of SC/ST to others*	
	SC	*ST*	*Other than SC/ST*	*SC*	*ST*
1991					
Male	49.91	40.65	69.53	19.62	28.88
Female	23.76	18.19	44.81	21.05	26.62
Total	37.41	29.6	57.69	20.28	28.09
2001					
Male	66.64	59.17	78.7	12.06	19.53
Female	41.9	34.76	58.17	16.27	23.41
Total	54.69	47.1	68.81	14.12	21.71
2011					
Male	75.2	68.5	80.9	5.7	12.4
Female	56.5	49.4	64.6	8.1	15.2
Total	66.1	59.0	73.0	6.9	14.0

Source: *Educational Statistics at a Glance*, Government of India, Ministry of Human Resource Development Bureau of Planning, Monitoring & Statistics, New Delhi, 2014, p. 22.

Table 2.9 Dropout rates, 2004–2005 and 2012–2013 – SC/ST (provisional)

	Class I–V			*Class I–VIII*			*Class I–X*		
Category	*All*	*Boys*	*Girls*	*All*	*Boys*	*Girls*	*All*	*Boys*	*Girls*
General	31.47	33.74	28.57	52.32	52.92	52.92	62.69	60.98	64.94
SC	32.7	36.1	34.2	55.2	57.3	57.3	69.1	74.2	71.3
2012–2013									
General	21.2	18.3	19.8	39.2	32.9	36.3	48.1	46.7	47.4
SC	17.7	15.4	16.6	42.4	34.4	38.8	51.8	48	50.1
ST	31.9	30.7	31.3	49.8	46.4	48.2	63.2	61.4	62.4

Source: Government of India XI Five Year Plan, 2007–2012, Vol. I, p. 105. And Educational Statistics at a Glance, Government of India, Ministry of Human Resource Development bureau of Planning, Monitoring & Statistics, New Delhi, 2014, p. 17.

2.9 Gross enrolment ratio in higher education

It follows from Table 2.10 that in the case of higher education the gross enrolment ratio in the case of all is registered as 21.1 in 2012–2013, while it is 15.1 in the case of SCs and 11 in the case of STs in the same year. There is a significant gap between the enrolment ratio of all classes and those of SC/STs.

Table 2.10 Gross Enrolment Ratio (GER), 2012–2013

	ALL			*SC*			*ST*		
	Boys	*Girls*	*Total*	*Boys*	*Girls*	*Total*	*Boys*	*Girls*	*Total*
Primary (I–V)	*98.1*	*100.6*	*99.3*	*110.8*	*112.2*	*111.5*	*111.5*	*108.8*	*110.2*
Upper Primary (VI–VIII)	84.9	90.3	87.4	93.2	96.5	94.8	86.5	85.7	86.1
Elementary (I–VIII)	93.3	96.9	95	104.2	109.4	102.8	102.5	100.5	101.5
Secondary (IX–X)	73.5	73.7	73.6	76	76.2	76.1	67.5	66.7	67.1
I–X	89.4	92.4	90.8	98.6	103	97.6	95.9	94.2	95.1
Senior	49.1	49.1	49.1	48.1	49.7	48.8	35.5	33.2	34.4
I–XII	83.3	85.9	84.6	91.1	93.3	92.2	87.5	86	86.8
Higher education	22.3	19.8	21.1	16	14.2	15.1	12.4	9.7	11

Source: *Educational Statistics at a Glance*, Government of India, Ministry of Human Resource Development bureau of Planning, Monitoring & Statistics, New Delhi, 2014.

Table 2.11 Enrolment of SC/ST students in higher education subject-wise (2005–2006)

Subjects	*Total*	*SC*	*ST*
Arts	4209248 (79.05)	645918 (15.35)	235608 (5.60)
Science	1809602 (85.14)	211058 (11.66)	57867 (3.20)
Commerce	1612171 (87.28)	149173 (9.25)	55918 (3.47)
Education	244825 (82.95)	32376 (13.22)	9372 (3.83)
Medicine	305629 (79.10)	44575 (14.58)	19316 (6.32)
Engineering	1668228 (81.82)	230085 (13.79)	73187 (4.39)
Agriculture &law	1464327 (86.31)	110674 (7.55)	90027 (6.14)
Others	2973517 (91.60)	183432 (6.17)	66299 (2.23)
Research	36019 (85.70)	3629 (10.08)	1520 (4.22)
TOTAL	14323566 (84.50)	1610920 (11.25)	609114 (4.25)

Source: *Selected Educational Statistics 2005–2006*, Ministry of Human Resource Development, Department of Education, Planning, Monitoring and Statistics Division, Government of India. (The figures in the brackets of the first column refer to percentages of others students (other than SC/ST).

2.10 Enrolment of SC/ST students in higher education subject-wise

It follows from Table 2.11 that of the total number of students 11.25% belongs to SC and 4.25% belong to ST while 84.50% belong to others (other than SC/STS) in 2005–2006. Out of the total number of arts students, 15.35% belong to SC, 5.6% belong to ST and 79.05% belong to others. 14.58% of medicine students belong to SC and 6.32% belong to ST while 79.10% medicine students belong to others. Similarly, 13.79% of engineering students belong to SCs and 4.39% engineering students belong to STs while 81.82% engineering students belongs to others. It is also to be noted that out of total number of research students 10.08% of students belong to SC and only 4.02% of students belong to ST while 85.70% of students belong to others.

It follows from the Table 2.12 that in 2005–2006 of 40%of the SC students in the arts, compared with 29% of the total students. In the case of ST students also about 39 percent are in arts. More than 14% of all SC students and 12% of all ST students are in engineering. About 15% of all ST students are in agriculture and law, compared with about 7% of all SC students and 10% of total students. The lowest percentage of all categories of students, 0.25% of total students, 0.22% of SCs students and 0.24% of ST students, are in research.

Table 2.12 SC/ST students in higher education subject-wise in number and percentage (2005–2006)

Subjects	*Total*	*SC (all students)*	*ST (all students)*	*Total women*	*SC women*	*ST women*
Arts	4209248 (29.39)	645918 (40.09)	235608 (38.68)	1841682 (12.86)	243546 (15.11)	86489 (14.19)
Science	1809602 (12.63)	211058 (13.10)	57867 (9.50)	752760 (5.26)	76504 (4.74)	20508 (3.36)
Commerce	1612171 (11.26)	149173 (9.26)	55918 (9.18)	636712 (4.45)	49828 (3.09)	22651 (3.71)
Education	244825 (1.71)	32376 (2.00)	9372 (1.53)	111557 (0.78)	13119 (0.81)	4054 (0.66)
Medicine	305629 (2.13)	44575 (2.76)	19316 (3.17)	144903 (1.01)	20561 (1.27)	8372 (1.37)
Engineering	1668228 (11.65)	230085 (14.2)	73187 (12.0)	593382 (4.14)	57028 (3.54)	19112 (3.13)
Agriculture &law	1464327 (10.12)	110674 (6.87)	90027 (14.77)	-	-	-
Others	2973517 (20.76)	183432 (11.38)	66299 (10.8)	1125126 (7.86)	81970 (5.08)	27256 (4.47)
Research	36019 (0.25)	3629 (0.22)	1520 (0.24)	14291 (0.10)	1163 (0.07)	760 (0.12)
TOTAL	14323566	1610920	609114	-	-	-

Source: *Selected Educational Statistics 2005–2006*, Ministry of Human Resource Development, Department of Education, Planning, Monitoring and Statistics Division, Government of India.

In the case of women students the highest percentage of SC women students, that is 15% and 14% of ST women students, are in the arts while about 13% of total students are in the arts. 3.54% of SC women students and 3.13% ST women students are in engineering, while 4.14% of total women students are in engineering. Only a negligible percentage of all categories of women students, that is, about 0.10% of students, are in research.

2.11 Public expenditure on education and Gross Domestic Product (GDP)

Table 2.13 shows that there has been an increase in the public expenditure on education as a percentage of GDP, from 0.64% in 1951 to 4.2% in 2012–2013. However, in India the share of public expenditure in GDP is desired to be more than 6%.

Table 2.14 shows the sector-wise expenditure on education at three points of time: that is, 2011, 2012 and 2013. There is a small change in the total expenditure on education as a percentage of GDP during the period 2011 to 2013, that is, from 4.05% in 2011 to 4.29% in 2013. It is also observed that among all the sectors of education, elementary education received the highest share at all the three points of time, that is, 1.7% of GDP in 2011, 1.76% of GDP in 2012 and 1.8% of GDP in 2013.

Table 2.13 Public expenditure on education and Gross Domestic Product (GDP)

Year	*GDP at Current price (at Factor cost) (Rs. crore)*	*Total Expenditure on Education by Education & other Departments (Rs. crore)*	*Expenditure on Education by Education & other Departments (% of GDP)*
1951–1952	10080	64.46	0.64
1960–1961	16220	239.56	1.48
1970–1971	42222	892.36	2.11
1980–1981	130178	3884.2	2.98
1990–1991	510964	19615.85	3.84
2000–2001	1925017	82486.48	4.28
2005–2006	3390503	113228.71	3.34
2006–2007	3953276	137383.99	3.48
2007–2008	4582086	155797.27	3.4
2008–2009	5303567	189068.84	3.56
2009–2010	6108903	241256.01	3.95
2010–2011	7248860	293478.23	4.05
2011–2012(RE)	8391691	351145.78	4.18
2012–2013(BE)	9388876	403236.51	4.2

Source: *Educational Statistics at a Glance*, Government of India, Ministry of Human Resource Development bureau of Planning, Monitoring & Statistics, New Delhi, 2014, p. 17.

Table 2.14 Expenditure on education by education and other departments by sector

2011	*Expenditure on Education (Rs. Crore)*			*Expenditure (as % of GDP)*		
Sector	*States/ UTs*	*Centre*	*Total*	*State/ UTs*	*Centre*	*Total*
Elementary Education	92337.49	31213.32	123550.8	1.27	0.43	1.7
Secondary Education	64220.73	7137.63	71358.36	0.89	0.1	0.98
University & Higher Education	38489.77	24164.41	62654.18	0.53	0.33	0.86
Adult Education	361.85	470.53	832.38	0	0.01	0.01
Technical Education	17407.67	17674.85	35082.52	0.24	0.24	0.48
Total (Education)	212817.5	80660.74	293478.3	2.94	1.11	4.05
2012						
Elementary Education	113874	34073.24	147947.2	1.36	0.41	1.76
Secondary Education	78529.58	9458.64	87988.22	0.94	0.11	1.05
University & Higher Education	44267.7	24786.96	69054.66	0.53	0.3	0.82
Adult Education	502.99	602.4	1105.39	0.01	0.01	0.01
Technical Education	24318.53	20731.74	45050.27	0.29	0.25	0.54

(*Continued*)

Table 2.14 (Continued)

2011	*Expenditure on Education (Rs. Crore)*			*Expenditure (as % of GDP)*		
Sector	*States/ UTs*	*Centre*	*Total*	*State/ UTs*	*Centre*	*Total*
Total (Education)	261492.8	89652.98	351145.8	3.12	1.07	4.18
2013						
Elementary Education	128228.1	41022.25	169250.4	1.37	0.44	1.8
Secondary Education	88376.15	10468.61	98844.76	0.94	0.11	1.05
University & Higher Education	50820.02	32739.21	83559.23	0.54	0.35	0.89
Adult Education	479.05	709.42	1188.47	0.01	0.01	0.01
Technical Education	26109.87	24283.82	50393.69	0.28	0.26	0.54
Total (Education)	294013.2	109223.3	403236.5	3.13	1.16	4.29

Source: *Educational Statistics at a Glance*, Government of India, Ministry of Human Resource Development Bureau of Planning, Monitoring & Statistics, New Delhi, 2014, p. 19.

2.12 Access to employment in government sector

From Table 2.15 it follows that there is some improvement in the SCs' representation in central government services during 1994–2013. But there is still a gap of 2% between their respective quota in group A and the actual number of positions occupied by SCs, even in 2013. In the case of STs there is a gap of about 3.5% between their respective quota and the actual number of positions occupied by them in Class I positions in 2004. The representation is found to be better in case of public enterprises with reference to SCs in 2013 (Table 2.16). However, in the case of group D in government services their quota was more than filled as jobs like sweeping and scavenging are usually not taken up by the others due to social stigma attached with such occupations.

2.13 Educational status across the different states in all social groups and among different social groups in India

2.13.1 Literacy Rates

It can be seen from Table 2.17 that in the case of total persons (rural + urban) the literacy rate is highest in Mizoram, that is, 91.58% followed by Tripura (87.75%) and Daman & Diu (87.07%), while it is the lowest in Bihar (63.82%), followed by Arunachal Pradesh (66.95%) and Rajasthan (67.06%).

In rural areas, the total literacy rate is highest in Mizoram (93.72%), followed by Tripura (92.18%) and Daman & Diu (91.49%), while it is lowest in Bihar (73.39%), followed by Arunachal Pradesh (73.69%) and

Table 2.15 Percentage of SC/STs representation in central government services in 1994, 1999, and 2004 (as on 1 January 2004)

	1994			*1999*			*2004*			*2013*		
Group	*Total*	*SCs*	%	*Total*	*SCs*	%	*Total*	*SCs*	%	*Total*	*SCs*	%
A	59016	6046	10.25	93520	10558	11.29	80011	9744	12.2	69157	9043	13.08
B	103198	12442	12.06	104963	13306	12.68	135409	19602	14.5	153584	24906	16.22
C	2381613	374758	15.73	2396426	378115	15.78	2040970	344865	16.9	2555461	438724	17.17
D	1023285	209423	20.47	949353	189761	19.99	802116	147212	18.4	111878	33536	29.98
Total	3567112	602670	16.9	3544262	591740	16.7	3058506	521423	17.05	2890080	506209	17.52
Group	Total	STs	%	Total	STs	%	Total	STs	%	Total	STs	%
A	59016	1727	2.92	93520	3172	3.39	80011	3311	4.1	-	-	-
B	103198	2902	2.81	104963	3512	2.35	135409	6,274	4.6	-	-	-
C	2381613	128228	5.38	2396426	145482	6.07	2040970	136630	6.7	-	-	-
D	1023285	62945	6.15	949353	66487	7	802116	53776	6.7	-	-	-
Total	3567112	195802	5.49	3544262	218653	6.17	3058506	199991	6.54	-	-	-

Source: 1. Government of India, *XI Five Year Plan, 2007–2012*, Volume I, p. 114. 2. National Commission for SCs, annual report, 2013–2014, p. 93.

Table 2.16 Representation of Scheduled Castes and Scheduled Tribes in central public sector enterprises as on 1 January 1996 and 01 January 2013

Group	*Total No. of Employees*	*No. of SC*	*%*	*No. of ST*	*%*	*No. of BC*	*%*
A	1,98,625	16,710	8.4	14505	2.27	-	-
B	1,64,402	15,921	9.68	5,788	3.52	-	-
C	1,32,860	2,16,801	19.14	98,816	8.72	-	-
D (excluding Safai Karamcharis)	4,77,254	1,06,934	22.41	50,958	10.68	-	-
Total	19,73,141	3,56,366	18.06	1,60,067	8.11	-	-
Safai Karamcharis	24,623	21,506	87.34	800	3.25	-	-
Total	19,97,764	3,77,872	18.91	1,60,867	8.05	-	-
2013							
A	162384	23751	14.63	-	-	19604	12.07
B	145356	21204	14.59	-	-	13553	9.32
C	465595	91786	19.71	-	-	80582	17.31
D (excluding Safai Karamcharis)	178494	364409	20.4	-	-	34002	19.05
Safai Karamcharis	7030	5412	76.98	-	-	411	5.85
Total	958859	718562		-	-	148152	

Source: National Commission for Scheduled Castes and Scheduled Tribes, *Fourth Report*, 1996–97 & 1997–1998, p. 176.

Andhra Pradesh (75.56%). In urban areas, the overall literacy rate is in highest Mizoram (89.4%), followed by Tripura (83.13%) and Chandigarh (81.38%), while it is the lowest in Rajasthan (52.66%), followed by Bihar (53.33%) and Jharkhand (56.21%)

In the case of the rural male literacy rate is highest in Tripura (90.86%), followed by Himachal Pradesh (90.48%) and the NCT of Delhi (90.04%), while it is lowest in Arunachal Pradesh (58.35%), followed by Andhra Pradesh (70.24%) and Bihar (71.0%). In terms of urban areas, the male literacy rate was at its highest in Mizoram (98.67%), followed by Tripura (95.8%) and Dadra & Nagar Haveli (78.18%), while it is lowest in Uttar Pradesh (81.75%), followed by Bihar (84.42%) and Jammu & Kashmir (84.9%). In the case of the rural female literacy rate, this is highest in Tripura (80.06%), followed by Mizoram (80.04%) and Himachal Pradesh (75.33%), while it is lowest in Rajasthan (46.25%), followed by Jharkhand (49.75%) and Bihar (50.82%). In urban areas, the female literacy rate is highest in Mizoram (97.54%), followed by Tripura (91.38%) and Meghalaya (89.49%), while it is lowest in Jammu & Kashmir (70.19%), followed by Rajasthan (71.58%) and Uttar Pradesh (71.68%).

Table 2.17 Literacy rate among all categories by sex and residence in India (as per 2011 Census) (Provisional)

	Literacy rate (Persons)			Literacy rate (Males)			Literacy rate (Females)		
States	*Total*	*Rural*	*Urban*	*Total*	*Rural*	*Urban*	*Total*	*Rural*	*Urban*
India	74.04	68.91	84.98	82.14	78.57	89.67	65.46	58.75	79.92
Jammu & Kashmir	68.74	64.97	78.19	78.26	75.51	84.9	58.01	53.36	70.19
Himachal Pradesh	83.78	82.91	91.39	90.83	90.48	93.72	76.6	75.33	88.66
Punjab	76.68	72.45	83.7	81.48	77.92	87.28	71.34	66.47	79.62
Chandigarh	86.43	81.69	86.56	90.54	86.68	90.65	81.38	74.17	81.55
Uttarakhand	79.63	77.11	85.2	88.33	87.63	89.78	70.7	66.79	80.02
Haryana	76.64	72.74	83.83	85.38	83.2	89.37	66.77	60.97	77.51
NCT Of Delhi	86.34	82.67	86.43	91.03	90.04	91.05	80.93	74.03	81.1
Rajasthan	67.06	62.34	80.73	80.51	77.49	89.16	52.66	46.25	71.53
Uttar Pradesh	69.72	67.55	77.01	79.24	78.48	81.75	59.26	55.61	71.68
Bihar	63.82	61.83	78.75	73.39	71.9	84.42	53.33	50.82	72.36
Sikkim	82.2	79.82	89.26	87.29	85.42	92.94	76.43	73.42	85.19
Arunachal Pradesh	66.95	61.59	84.57	73.69	68.79	89.45	59.57	53.78	79.04
Nagaland	80.11	75.86	90.21	83.29	79.49	92.11	76.69	72.01	88.1
Manipur	79.85	77.15	85.98	86.49	84.14	92.05	73.17	69.95	80.21
Mizoram	91.58	84.31	98.1	93.72	88.35	98.67	89.4	80.04	97.54
Tripura	87.75	85.58	93.61	92.18	90.86	95.8	83.15	80.06	91.38
Meghalaya	75.48	71.15	91.33	77.17	72.83	93.17	73.78	69.45	89.49
Assam	73.18	70.44	88.88	78.81	76.51	91.84	67.27	64.09	85.71
West Bengal	77.08	72.97	85.54	82.67	79.51	89.15	71.16	66.08	81.7
Jharkhand	67.63	62.4	83.3	78.45	74.57	89.78	56.21	49.75	76.17
Orissa	73.45	70.78	86.45	82.4	80.41	91.83	64.36	61.1	80.7
Chhattisgarh	71.04	66.76	84.79	81.45	78.2	91.63	60.59	55.4	77.65
Madhya Pradesh	70.63	65.29	84.09	80.53	76.64	90.24	60.02	53.2	77.39
Gujarat	79.31	73	87.58	87.23	83.1	92.44	70.73	62.41	82.08
Daman & Diu	87.07	81.51	88.87	91.48	89.71	91.95	79.59	71.97	82.94
Dadra & Nagar Haveli	77.65	65.89	90.86	86.46	78.18	94.81	65.93	51.36	84.86
Maharashtra	82.91	77.09	89.84	89.82	86.39	93.79	75.48	67.38	85.44
Andhra Pradesh	67.66	61.14	80.54	75.56	70.24	85.99	59.74	52.05	75.02

Source: Population Census, 2011.

2.14 State-wise Scheduled Tribe literacy rate

It can be seen from Table 2.18 that the literacy rate, in the case of total ST persons, is highest in Lakshadweep (91.7%), followed by Mizoram (91.51%) and Nagaland (80.04), while it is lowest in Andhra Pradesh (49.21%), followed by Jammu and Kashmir (50.56%) and Madhya Pradesh (50.55).

In rural areas, the total STs literacy rate is highest in Lakshadweep (91.5%), followed by Mizoram (84.48%) and Daman & Diu (79.65%), while it is

Table 2.18 State-wise Scheduled Tribe literacy rate by residence and sex in India (as per 2011 census)

	Person			*Male*			*Female*		
States/UTs	*Total*	*Rural*	*Urban*	*Total*	*Rural*	*Urban*	*Total*	*Rural*	*Urban*
Andaman and Nicobar	75.58	74.21	95.21	80.87	79.75	97.96	69.92	68.23	92.61
Andhra Pradesh	49.21	46.88	66.82	58.35	56.15	74.72	40.09	37.66	58.72
Arunachal Pradesh	64.58	60.37	84.59	71.48	67.65	90.34	57.96	53.3	79.38
Assam	72.06	70.95	90.04	78.96	78.04	93.75	65.1	63.77	86.35
Bihar	51.08	50.32	65.33	61.31	60.7	72.5	40.38	39.47	57.62
Chhattisgarh	59.09	57.57	76.94	69.67	68.36	84.92	48.76	47.06	68.97
Dadra and Nagar Haveli	61.85	58.46	79.53	73.62	70.84	88.03	50.27	46.3	71.1
Daman and Diu	78.79	79.65	77.96	86.23	87.47	85.03	71.23	71.74	70.73
Goa	79.14	78.39	80.19	87.16	86.36	88.32	71.53	70.68	72.71
Gujarat	62.48	61.29	72.71	71.68	70.7	79.96	53.16	51.79	65.13
Himachal Pradesh	73.64	72.96	87.39	83.17	82.69	92.48	64.2	63.36	81.94
Jammu& Kashmir	50.56	49.14	71.68	60.58	59.27	79.57	39.73	38.27	62.57
Jharkhand	57.13	55.22	75.44	68.17	66.6	83.22	46.2	43.94	67.78
Karnataka	62.08	58.99	74.82	71.14	68.54	81.88	52.98	49.39	67.75
Kerala	75.81	74.05	90.35	80.76	79.35	92.67	71.08	68.96	88.21
Lakshadweep	91.7	91.5	91.75	95.69	94.69	95.97	87.76	88.33	87.61
Madhya Pradesh	50.55	49.32	66.73	59.55	58.43	73.99	41.47	40.15	59.16
Maharashtra	65.73	63.21	80.28	74.27	72.18	86.1	57.02	54.13	74.13
Manipur	77.36	75.89	87.67	82.08	80.75	91.64	72.71	71.05	83.94
Meghalaya	74.53	70.98	91.26	75.54	72.19	92.31	73.55	69.77	90.33
Mizoram	91.51	84.48	97.92	93.59	88.57	98.37	89.47	80.25	97.5
Nagaland	80.04	76.04	92.59	83.11	79.54	94.57	76.91	72.43	90.64
Odisha	52.24	51.08	69.08	63.7	62.72	77.67	41.2	39.91	60.46
Rajasthan	52.8	51.73	68.99	67.62	66.7	81.03	37.27	36.1	55.57
Sikkim	79.74	77.48	89.15	85.01	83.21	92.9	74.27	71.39	85.58
Tamil Nadu	54.34	51.32	69.1	61.81	59.02	75.4	46.8	43.55	62.7
Tripura	79.05	78.44	92.22	86.43	86.05	94.8	71.59	70.73	89.7
Uttar Pradesh	55.68	54.48	66.97	67.08	66.23	74.81	43.72	42.28	58.02
Uttarakhand	73.88	72.39	88.33	83.56	82.49	93.73	63.89	61.97	82.63
West Bengal	57.93	56.68	71.22	68.17	67.21	78.4	47.71	46.19	64.01
India	58.96	56.89	76.78	68.53	66.82	83.16	49.35	46.93	70.32

Source: Population Census, 2011.

at its lowest in Andhra Pradesh(46.88%), followed by Jammu & Kashmir (49.14%) and Madhya Pradesh (49.32%). In urban areas, total STs literacy rate is highest in Mizoram (97.92%), followed by Andaman and Nicobar (95.21%) and Nagaland (92.59%), while it is lowest in Bihar (65.33%), followed by Madhya Pradesh (66.73%) and Andhra Pradesh (66.82%).

In the case of STs male literacy rate (rural + urban) Lakshadweep has registered highest (95.69%), followed by Mizoram (93.59%) and Goa (87.16%), while it is lowest in Andhra Pradesh (58.35%), followed by Madhya Pradesh (59.55%) and Jammu & Kashmir (60.55%).

In rural areas, the STs male literacy rate Lakshadweep has the highest percentage (94.69%), followed by Mizoram (88.57%) and Daman & Diu (87.47%), while it is lowest in Andhra Pradesh (56.15%), followed by Madhya Pradesh (58.43%) and Tamil Nadu (59.02%). In urban areas, the STs male literacy rate is highest in Mizoram (98.37%), followed by Andaman and Nicobar (97.96%) and Lakshadweep (95.97%), while it is lowest in Bihar (72.1%), followed by Madhya Pradesh (73.99%) and Andhra Pradesh (74.72%). In rural areas the STs female literacy rate Lakshadweep has the highest percentage (88.33%), followed by Mizoram (80.25) and Nagaland (72.43%), while it is lowest in Rajasthan (36.1%), followed by Andhra Pradesh (37.66%) and Jammu & Kashmir (38.27%). In urban areas, the STs female literacy rate in Andaman and Nicobar has registered the highest percentage (92.61%), followed by Mizoram (97.5%) and Nagaland (90.64%), while it is lowest in Rajasthan (55.57%), followed by Bihar (57.62%) and Uttar Pradesh (58.02%).

Finally, in the case of the STs female literacy rate (rural + urban), Mizoram has registered the highest percentage (89.47%), followed by Lakshadweep (87.76%) and Nagaland (76.91%), while it is lowest in Rajasthan (37.27%), followed by Jammu & Kashmir (39.73%) and Andhra Pradesh (40.09%).

2.15 State-wise Scheduled Caste literacy rate

It can be seen from Table 2.19 that the literacy rate, in the case of total SC persons, is highest in Daman & Diu (92.56), followed by Mizoram (92.43) and Tripura (89.45), while it is lowest in Bihar (48.65%),followed by Jharkhand (55.89) and Rajasthan (59.75).

In rural areas, the total SCs literacy rate is highest in Daman & Diu (93.23%), followed by Tripura (89.1%) and Kerala (87.21%), while it is lowest in Bihar (47.66%), followed by Jharkhand (52.72%) and Rajasthan (57.17%). In urban areas, the total SCs literacy rate is highest in Mizoram (95.61%), followed by Daman & Diu (92.19%) and Dadra & Nagar Haveli (91.22%), while it is lowest in Uttar Pradesh (67.47%), followed by Jharkhand (67.34%) and Uttar Pradesh (67.47%).

In the case of the SCs male literacy rate (rural + urban) Daman & Diu has the highest percentage (96.79%), followed by Dadra & Nagar Haveli (93.11%) and Mizoram (93.08%), while it is lowest in Bihar (57.97%),

Table 2.19 State-wise Scheduled Caste literacy rate by residence and sex in India (as per 2011 Census)

	Persons			*Male*			*Female*		
States/UTs	*Total*	*Rural*	*Urban*	*Total*	*Rural*	*Urban*	*Total*	*Rural*	*Urban*
Andhra Pradesh	62.28	58.65	75.2	70.23	66.97	81.99	54.44	50.39	68.64
Assam	76.99	75.66	82.75	83.17	82.1	87.89	70.45	68.82	77.41
Bihar	48.65	47.66	60.64	57.97	57.05	68.96	38.46	37.41	51.35
Chandigarh	76.45	68.5	76.65	83.57	76.64	83.75	68.27	57.91	68.51
Chhattisgarh	70.76	68.97	76.57	81.66	80.48	85.48	59.86	57.46	67.61
Dadra & Nagar Haveli	89.42	82.82	91.22	93.11	88.43	94.57	85.03	74.24	87.49
Daman & Diu	92.56	93.23	92.19	96.79	97.73	96.27	88.09	88.52	87.84
Goa	83.73	81.41	85.13	89.9	88.42	90.77	77.69	74.71	79.51
Gujarat	79.18	75.18	84.17	87.87	85.36	90.98	69.87	64.39	76.79
Haryana	66.85	65.75	69.78	75.93	75.1	78.14	56.65	55.2	60.46
Himachal Pradesh	78.92	78.33	86.43	86.23	85.85	90.93	71.46	70.7	81.48
Jammu & Kashmir	70.16	68.27	78.04	78.79	77.28	84.9	60.67	58.47	70.12
Jharkhand	55.89	52.72	67.34	66.94	64.05	77.25	44.2	40.78	56.68
Karnataka	65.33	60.44	77.43	74.03	69.98	84.08	56.58	50.82	70.76
Kerala	88.73	87.21	90.98	92.64	91.5	94.33	85.07	83.19	87.85
Madhya Pradesh	66.16	62.72	75.13	76.72	74.05	83.71	54.7	50.39	65.88
Maharashtra	79.66	75.79	84.64	87.18	84.61	90.49	71.89	66.63	78.6
Manipur	76.21	72.67	79.59	83.53	80.67	86.31	68.91	64.53	73.01
Meghalaya	68.57	61.14	82.77	74.89	67.94	88.17	61.43	53.45	76.67
Mizoram	92.43	81.96	95.61	93.08	85.79	95.54	91.04	70.77	95.73
NCT of Delhi	78.89	77.18	78.94	86.77	86.72	86.77	70.01	66.34	70.12
Odisha	69.02	68.05	75.18	79.21	78.45	83.97	58.76	57.59	66.23
Puducherry	77.9	73.87	83.04	85.22	81.82	89.57	71.05	66.42	76.94
Punjab	64.81	62.98	69.78	70.66	68.94	75.3	58.39	56.47	63.66
Rajasthan	59.75	57.17	68.64	73.77	71.8	80.58	44.63	41.4	55.78
Sikkim	77.54	74.35	85.43	82.8	79.88	90.3	72.04	68.42	80.6
Tamil Nadu	73.26	69.91	79.6	80.94	78.22	86.14	65.64	61.66	73.17
Tripura	89.45	89.1	90.14	92.78	92.57	93.2	85.98	85.45	87.02
Uttar Pradesh	60.89	59.8	67.47	71.77	71.12	75.65	48.87	47.35	58.2
Uttarakhand	74.41	73.12	79.12	84.34	83.81	86.23	64.05	62.14	71.29
West Bengal	69.43	67.53	76.72	77.22	75.7	83.06	61.23	58.93	70.04
India	66.07	62.85	76.17	75.17	72.58	83.32	56.46	52.56	68.64

Source: Population Census, 2011.

followed by Jharkhand (66.94%) and Andhra Pradesh (70.23%). In rural areas, the SC male literacy rate Daman & Diu has registered highest (97.73%), followed by Tripura (92.57%) and Kerala (91.5%), while it is lowest in Bihar (57.05%), followed by Jharkhand (64.05%) and Andhra Pradesh (66.97%). In urban areas, the SC male literacy rate is highest in Daman & Diu is highest (96.27%), followed by Mizoram (95.54%) and

Dadra & Nagar Haveli (94.57%), while it is lowest in Bihar (68.96%), followed by Punjab (75.3%) and Uttar Pradesh (75.65%).

In the case of SCs the female literacy rate (rural + urban) Mizoram has registered the highest percentage (91.04%), followed by Daman & Diu (88.09%) and Tripura (85.98%), while it is lowest in Bihar (38.46%), followed by Jharkhand (44.2%) and Rajasthan (44.63%).

2.16 State-wise dropout rates

Table 2.20 presents the dropout rate (I–X Class) is highest in Assam (77.4%), followed by Nagaland (75.1%) and Sikkim (69.9&) in the case of all categories in 2009–2010 while the dropout rate is lowest in Puducherry (6.6%), followed by Himachal Pradesh (16%) and Haryana (18.9%) during the same period. In the case of girls the dropout rate is highest (I–X) in Assam (78.1%), followed by Meghalaya (76.7%) and Nagaland (74.4), while it is lowest in Pondicherry (1.5%), followed by Uttar Pradesh (14.4%) and Haryana (16%). In the case of boys, the dropout rate is highest (I–X) in Assam (76.8%), followed by Nagaland (75.8%) and Sikkim (72.4%), while it is lowest in Himachal Pradesh (15.2), followed by Delhi (19.7%).

2.17 State-wise dropout rates (SC)

It can be seen from Table 2.21 that the dropout rate (I–X Class) is highest in Bihar (79.8%), followed by Meghalaya (78.9%) and Sikkim (75.2%) in the case of total SCs in 2009–2010, while the dropout rate is lowest in Kerala (6.2%), followed by Puducherry (8%) and Tamil Nadu (10.7%) during the same period. In the case of SC girls, dropout rates are highest (I–X) in Meghalaya (80.4%), followed by Bihar (79.8%) and Rajasthan (78.4), while it is lowest in Pondicherry (0.5%), then followed by Kerala (2.9%) and Haryana (16.3%). In the case of SC, the boys dropout rate is highest (I–X) in Bihar (79.8%), followed by Odisha (77.7%) and Sikkim (77.2%), while it is lowest in Kerala (9.3%), followed by Puducherry (15%) and Haryana (17.6%).

2.18 State-wise dropout rates (ST)

It can be seen from Table 2.22 that the dropout rate (I–X Class) is highest in Odisha (85.6%), followed by Meghalaya (79.6%) and West Bengal (74.6%) in 2009–2010, while it is lowest In Himachal Pradesh (2.1%), followed by Kerala (29.1%) and Tamil Nadu (31.9%) during the same period in the case of total STs. In the case of ST boys, the dropout rate is highest in Odisha (86.4%), followed by Meghalaya (81.3%) and Jharkhand (80.8%), while it is the lowest in Himachal Pradesh (0.3%), followed by Andaman & Nicobar (28.7%) and Kerala (31.8%) in 2009–2010. In the case of ST girls' dropout rate, the figure is highest in Odisha (84.5%), followed by Rajasthan (80.7%) and Jharkhand (78.4%), while it is lowest in Himachal Pradesh (4.1%), followed by Lakshadweep (22.9%) and Kerala (27.1%).

Table 2.20 State-wise dropout rates (all categories) in 2009–2010

States/Union Territories	*Classes I–V*			*Classes I–VIII*			*Classes I–X*		
	Boys	*Girls*	*Total*	*Boys*	*Girls*	*Total*	*Boys*	*Girls*	*Total*
Andhra Pradesh	18.1	16.7	17.4	33	32.7	32.9	45.8	46.6	46.2
Arunachal Pradesh	43.8	42.1	43	51.7	49.1	50.5	62.3	61	61.7
Assam	33.2	26.4	29.9	49.8	58.2	54	76.8	78.1	77.4
Bihar	39.2	30.7	35.7	58.5	58	58.3	64.4	58.9	62.2
Chhattisgarh	29.7	32.2	31	47.7	49	48.3	58.4	57.5	58
Goa	-	2.4	-	-	-	-	29.3	26.9	28.1
Gujarat	36.9	6.6	25.7	44.6	49.4	46.7	61.1	52.4	57.9
Haryana	9.8	8.9	9.4	5.3	3.9	4.6	21.2	16	18.9
Himachal Pradesh	3.9	3.6	3.8	-	-	-	15.2	17	16
Jammu	9.8	6.8	8.4	7.8	4	6.1	47.1	38.9	43.6
Jharkhand	31	25.6	28.4	48.4	41.2	45.1	70.6	68.1	69.5
Karnataka	9.2	8.5	8.9	20.1	21.5	20.8	44.5	42.1	43.3
Kerala	-	-	-	-	-	-	-	-	-
Madhya	33.5	25	29.5	34	27	30.7	44.3	59.3	51.1
Maharashtra	21.4	19	20.3	24.5	27.4	25.9	36.5	40	38.2
Manipur	46.1	45.3	45.7	51.7	53.9	52.8	45.7	44.8	45.3
Meghalaya	61	55.7	58.4	72.5	68.3	70.4	78	76.7	77.4
Mizoram	37.1	38.7	37.9	37.5	35.7	36.7	55	52.3	53.7
Nagaland	40.1	39.8	39.9	45.2	45.6	45.4	75.8	74.4	75.1
Odisha	11	2.4	7	54.4	55.6	55	67.2	59.7	64
Punjab	-	-	-	-	-	-	30.2	30.7	30.5
Rajasthan	49.9	51.5	50.6	49.2	58.1	53.3	68.2	69	68.5
Sikkim	24.9	11	18.4	50.6	34.3	42.8	72.4	67.1	69.9
Tamil	-	-	-	7.8	8.2	8	28.2	23.6	25.9
Tripura	31.9	30.3	31.1	50.2	45.9	48.2	59.1	57.5	58.4
Uttar Pradesh	33.5	34.8	34.1	49.3	50.2	49.7	29.8	14.4	24
Uttarakhand	33.5	32.2	32.9	33.7	29.3	31.6	31.8	41.3	36.6
West Bengal	29.8	27	28.4	50.4	47.7	49.1	64.9	63.5	64.2
Andaman and Nicobar	8.4	7.1	7.8	13.2	17.1	15.1	19.2	23.3	21.1
Dadra & Nagar Haveli	9.1	16.5	12.7	27.4	40.2	33.7	51.7	58.3	54.7
Daman	8.5	8	8.3	13.1	8.3	10.8	26.7	30.2	28.3
Delhi	3.7	8.5	5.9	-	-	-	19.7	26.3	22.9
Lakshadweep	10.8	3.1	7.1	15.5	9.7	12.7	41.1	20.3	31.3
Puducherry	-	-	-	-	-	-	10.9	1.4	6.4
India	28.7	25.1	27	40.3	41	40.6	50.4	47.9	49.3

Sources: Statistics of School Education, 2010–2011.

2.19 Summary and conclusion

Under the Peshwas, the depressed classes were entirely beyond the pale of education. The British were silent for a long time on the question of promoting education among the native population. In the Bombay Presidency no schools were opened for depressed classes before 1855; this was because the deliberate policy of the British government was to restrict the

Table 2.21 State-wise dropout rates (SC) in 2009–2010

States/Union Territories	Classes I–V			Classes I–VIII			Classes I–X		
	Boys	Girls	Total	Boys	Girls	Total	Boys	Girls	Total
Andhra Pradesh	20.2	19	19.6	36.1	35.6	35.9	49.7	49.7	49.7
Arunachal Pradesh	100	100	100	100	100	100	100	100	100
Assam	28.8	23.4	26.2	39.4	48.8	44	-	-	-
Bihar	40.9	35.9	38.8	64	58.6	61.9	79.8	79.9	79.8
Chhattisgarh	42.3	47	44.7	50.3	46.9	48.7	57.6	60.5	59
Goa	9.8	20.9	15.1	-	-	-	53.4	46	49.8
Gujarat	47.4	42.7	45.2	47.9	58.5	52.9	60.4	69.3	64.5
Haryana	3.4	0.9	2.2	15.3	10.4	13	17.6	16.4	17
Himachal Pradesh	6.8	7.8	7.3	6.2	10.5	8.3	32.1	33	32.5
Jammu	-	-	-	16.6	2.7	10	-	-	-
Jharkhand	42	39	40.6	44.5	35.8	40.8	73.7	70.2	72.3
Karnataka	14.4	14.3	14.3	28	31.8	29.9	54.1	57.1	55.6
Kerala	-	-	-	-	-	-	9.3	2.9	6.2
Madhya	32.9	24.5	28.9	19.5	14.6	17.1	32.1	57.2	43.2
Maharashtra	24.9	20.2	22.7	21.7	24.2	22.9	35.3	41.5	38.3
Manipur	29.6	28.9	29.3	51.4	41.8	46.8	-	-	-
Meghalaya	15.5	20.2	17.7	69.4	72.2	70.8	76.2	80.4	78.3
Mizoram	-	-	-	50	-	-	-	-	-
Odisha	16.6	14.8	15.7	58.3	59.8	59	77.7	71.4	75.1
Punjab	7.3	12.6	9.8	-	-	-	57.3	54	55.7
Rajasthan	49.8	51.4	50.5	55.1	62.9	58.6	71.5	78.4	74.5
Sikkim	34.6	28.8	31.9	72.7	61.5	67.5	77.2	73.2	75.2
Tamil Nadu	-	0.3	-	-	-	-	28.9	-	10.7
Tripura	16.6	13.8	15.3	29.9	24	27	47.1	48.5	47.8
Uttar	33.8	15.1	26	66	44.8	58.7	60.9	50.4	57.2
Uttarakhand	29.9	25.5	27.8	36.6	37.4	37	45.4	55	50.2
West	25.9	26	25.9	50	51.9	50.9	68.5	63.7	66.2
Chandigarh	-	-	-	-	-	-	45.7	40.6	43.3
Dadra & Nagar Haveli	16.9	11.1	14.6	15.4	11.8	13.5	32.4	23.1	28.1
Daman	6.6	-	1.8	-	-	-	-	-	-
Delhi	23.5	6.1	16.3	42.9	37.1	40.1	-	-	-
Lakshadweep	-	-	-	-	-	-	-	100	100
Puducherry	-	-	-	-	-	-	15	0.5	8
India	29.8	23.1	26.7	46.7	39	43.3	57.4	54.1	56

Sources: Statistics of School Education 2010–2011.

benefits of higher education to the higher castes, chiefly the Brahmins and the other upper classes. However, from 1854 onwards measures were taken to spread mass education to the whole of the country. The results of this policy were first examined by the Hunter Commission in 1982. Although the policy was mass education, following the reforms the masses were every bit as excluded as they were before 1854 and the lowest classes of Hindus

Table 2.22 State-wise dropout rates (ST) in 2009–2010

States/Union Territories	Classes I–V			Classes I–VIII			Classes I–X		
	Boys	Girls	Total	Boys	Girls	Total	Boys	Girls	Total
Andhra Pradesh	35.5	38.2	36.8	60.5	64.5	62.5	71.6	73.8	72.7
Arunachal Pradesh	44.6	42.7	43.7	54.4	48.4	51.6	63.6	63.3	63.5
Assam	26.8	24.5	25.7	49.7	57.1	53.4	-	-	-
Bihar	31.6	19.8	27.1	59.1	47	54.8	72.2	69	71.1
Chhattisgarh	38.4	42.1	40.3	45.4	49.5	47.4	63.3	62	62.7
Gujarat	50.9	44.6	48	69.4	71.2	70.2	79.7	75.2	77.6
Himachal Pradesh	0	-	-	-	-	-	0.3	4.1	2.1
Jammu	27.9	31.9	29.8	58.5	68	62.7	-	-	-
Jharkhand	39.6	35	37.5	60.5	49.4	55.8	80.8	78.5	79.8
Karnataka	6.9	6.9	6.9	24.2	29.7	26.9	47.5	48.3	47.9
Kerala	-	-	-	9.1	8.5	8.8	31.2	27.1	29.1
Madhya	40.6	33.3	37.1	38.6	33.4	36.1	58.7	71.9	64.6
Maharashtra	23.7	17.9	21.1	42.3	46.8	44.4	65.7	74.5	69.8
Manipur	47.5	55.4	51.3	74.3	75.7	75	-	-	-
Meghalaya	57.5	51.5	54.6	75.7	72	73.8	81.3	77.8	79.6
Mizoram	37.6	39.2	38.4	38.2	36.5	37.4	55.5	52.6	54.1
Nagaland	40.5	39	39.8	43.4	38.4	41.1	70.3	66.5	68.5
Odisha	25.2	18.6	22.1	74	75.3	74.6	86.4	84.5	85.6
Rajasthan	47.8	51.2	49.4	59.5	68.9	64	78.2	80.7	79.3
Sikkim	26.8	11.1	19.1	55.5	39.1	47.5	59.3	44.7	52.2
Tamil Nadu	4.4	-	-	5.6	-	-	34.2	29.2	31.9
Tripura	41.6	41.5	41.5	60.4	62.8	61.6	71	72.2	71.6
Uttar Pradesh	-	-	-	27.9	13.8	22.2	-	-	-
Uttarakhand	21.5	9.9	16.3	34	29.2	31.6	34.1	37.7	36
West Bengal	31.4	24.8	28.3	49.4	46.9	48.2	77.3	70.9	74.6
Andaman & Nicobar	1.7	-	0.2	23	27	24.9	28.7	35	31.9
Chandigarh	-	-	-	100	100	100	-	-	-
Dadra & Nagar Haveli	1.3	21.3	12	34.2	48.8	41.6	60.2	66.8	63.3
Daman	2	7.9	5	10.6	33.6	21.9	-	-	-
Delhi	24.6	23.5	24.1	-	-	-	-	-	-
Lakshadweep	12.7	5	9	16.8	11.3	14.1	43.3	22.9	33.6
Puducherry	-	-	-	-	-	-	-	-	-
India	37.2	33.9	35.6	54.7	55.4	55	70.6	71.3	70.9

Source: Statistics of School Education 2010–2011.

remains lowest in the order of education. After the year 1882, the year 1923 from the next landmark in the educational history of Bombay as that year marks the transfer of primary education from the control of provincial governments to the control of local bodies. The depressed classes, who are second in order of population, stand fourth, i.e., last, in the order of college education, last in the order of secondary education and last in the order of primary education in 1923.

Dr. Ambedkar argued in the Bombay legislative council in 1927 that the government should see that education reaches everybody and expenditure on education should be increased. He opposed the commercialisation of education. He viewed education as not only an important instrument of economic development and agent of social change but also equip Dalits to fight for their human rights. He also argued that if unequal communities are to be brought to the level of equality the only remedy is to adopt the principle of inequality and to give favoured treatment to those who are below the level.

After attaining independence particularly from 1stFive Year Plan onwards various developmental measures were initiated in addition to general developmental programmes for the social and economic development of Dalits (SC/ST). There has been a significant improvement in the literacy rates of SCs, STs and general population in the post-Independence period. However, there is a significant gap between literacy rate of SCs/STs and general population in 2011. When we examine the literacy rate across the states/UTs, in case of total SC persons, it is highest in Daman & Diu (92.56%), followed by Mizoram (92.43%) and Tripura (89.45%) while it is lowest in Bihar (48.65%), followed by Jharkhand (55.89%) and Rajasthan (59.75%).

The dropout rate has significantly declined with regard to all categories from class I–X during 2004–2005 to 2012–2013. However, the dropout rates are higher in the case of SC/STs compared to the general population. In higher education, the Gross Enrolment Ratio (GER) in the case of all classes is 21.1, while it is 15.1 in the case of SCs and 11 in the case of STs in 2012–2013. That is, there is a significant gap between SC/STs and total population in terms of their access to higher education. It is also noted that the SC/STs students are mostly concentrated in arts/humanities/social sciences then in engineering in 2012–2013.

Regarding the expenditure on education there has been an improvement in terms of GDP during 1951–1952 to 2012–2013. It was 4.2% of GDP in 2012–2013. However, it is required to be increased to 6% of GDP and special measures to be strengthened for the educational development of SC/STs. Among various sectors of education, elementary education receives the highest share i.e. 1.8% of GDP in 2013.

Regarding representation of SC/STs in central government employment there is some gap with respect to group A positions in the case of SCs in 2012–2013 and in the case of STs in 2004 between their respective quota and the positions actually occupied by them. Therefore, the government should strictly implement the reservation policy to bridge the gap.

References

Government of Maharashtra, Education Department. (1982). *Dr. Babasaheb Ambedkar Writings &Speeches*, Vol. 2.

Government of Maharashtra, Education Department. (1993). *Dr.Babasaheb Ambedkar: Writings and Speeches*, Vol. 12.

Primary Census Abstract for Total Population, Scheduled Castes and Scheduled Tribes. (2011). Office of the Registrar General & Census Commissioner, New Delhi.

Shahare, M.L. (1991). *Dr. B. R. Ambedkar: An Eminent Educationist in (Edit.) Sudarshan Agarwal, Dr. B. R. Ambedkar: The Man and Message, A Commemorative Volume*. Prentice Hall of India, Private Limited, New Delhi. pp. 134–138.

3 Land, labour, poverty and Dalits

Post-independence period

3.1 Introduction

This chapter attempts to study the changes in the occupational distribution of the workforce and access to land with special reference to Dalits (SCs/STs) at both the national and state levels in the context of land reform and agricultural growth in the post-Independence period. This chapter also attempts to understand the linkages between Dalits' dependence on agriculture as landless labour and the high incidence of poverty among this group. The analysis is based on secondary data obtained from various NSSO reports and the population census compiled by the Government of India. Some village studies are also employed to give an understanding of the process of land transfers in rural India. Further, this chapter examines the changes in the incidence of poverty among different social groups with special reference to Dalits in the post-Independence period.

3.2 Agriculture and Dalits

According to the 2011 Census, SC constitutes 16.6% of the total population and STs constitute 8.6% of the total population at the all-India level. The maximum concentration of the SC population is in Uttar Pradesh, followed by West Bengal, Bihar, Andhra Pradesh and Tamil Nadu. These five states together account for nearly 55 per cent of the SC population in India. 68% of ST Population live in seven major states, Chattisgarh, Jharkhand, Orissa, Madhya Pradesh, Maharashtra, Gujarat and Rajasthan. 24% of the SC population and 10% of the ST population live in urban areas as against 35.% of the non-SC/ST population. That is, about 76% of the SC population and about 90% of the ST population live in rural areas, as against 65% of the non-SC/ST population.

The work participation rate of SCs, defined as the percentage of SC population participating in the workforce to total Scheduled Caste population, is 40.87% and that of STs is 48.72% as against 34% among others in 2011. The high participation rate among SCs and STs is due to the very high participation rate among SC women (33.6%) and among ST women (55.5%) as against 30% for the other women population of the country. (Census, 2011).

DOI: 10.4324/9781003147053-3

In view of the heavy dependence of SCs and STs on agriculture, now let us examine the changes in agrarian structure and agrarian relations in the context of land reform and agricultural growth with special reference to Dalits.

3.3 Share of Dalits and others in land owned

From Table 3.1 it follows that SC households constituted about 20% of total rural households, but that they control only about 8% of the total area owned, while other households constitute about 70% of total rural households, but control approximately 82% of total area owned in 1982. By 1992, the percentage of SC rural households increased to more than 21% and their share in land also increased to 10%, while the percentage of other households in terms of land ownership is better than that of SC households. By 2003, the percentage of SC rural households remained at 21.58%, but their share in the land owned declined to 9.04% while other households which constitute 67.87% of total households control 79.81% total land owned. And by 2013, SC households accounted for 20.06% of total households but control only 8.52% of total area owned while other households, which constitute 23.23%, control 32.02% of total land.

In 1982, the ST households constitute 9.7% of total rural households and control 10% of the total area owned. However, the quality of land

Table 3.1 Share of Scheduled Caste and Scheduled Tribe households in total area owned and landlessness among them (Rural in %)

		SOCIAL GROUP				
ITEM	*YEAR*	*SC*	*ST*	*OBC*	*OTHERS**	*ALL HOUSE-HOLDS*
(1)	(2)	(3)	(4)	5	(6)	(7)
1. Percentage of distribution of households	1982	19.7	9.7	-	70.6	100
	1992	21.5	11.2	-	67.4	100
	2003	21.58	10.55	-	67.87	100
	2013	20.06	11.89	44.82	23.23	100
2. Percentage of distribution of area owned	1982	7.9	10.1	-	82.0	100
	1992	10.2	11.8	-	78.0	100
	2003	9.04	11.15	-	79.81	100
	2013	8.52	12.06	45.68	32.02	100
3. Percentage of landless households owning no land less than 0.02 ha.	1982	12.6	17.1	-	10.2	11.3
	1992	13.3	11.5	-	10.5	11.3
	2003	11.31	12.81	-	9.51	10.03
	2013	7.18	9.41	6.98	14.2	7.41

* Other refers to non-SC/ST up to 2003. In 2013 other refers to Non-SC/ST/OBC

Source: NSSO Report No. 399 (48th round, January–December 1992) 1997, p. 33 & XIth Five Year Plan, Vol. I. NSSO Report No. 571 (70th round, January–December 2013 p. 28).

owned by ST households is inferior to that of land owned by others and their agricultural productivity is very low. By 1992, their households percentage increased to more than 11%, while their share in area owned increased to nearly 11%. By 2003, the percentage of ST households declined to 10.55 and their share in land remains almost same, at 11.15%. In 2013, ST households accounted for 11.89% of total households, accounting for 13.06%of total area owned. OBC households registered 44.82% of total households, but control 45.68% of total area owned in 2013.

3.4 Landlessness among the Dalits and others

It is also seen from Table 3.1 that landlessness is more prevalent among SC households. The percentage of landless households was 12.6%, while the corresponding percentages among the other rural households was 10.2% in 1982. By 1992, the percentage of SC landless households increased to 13.3% while in the case of other households landlessness, remained at 10.2%.

The percentage of landless households declined to 11.31% in 2003 and declined further to 7.18% in 2013. Among ST households, the percentage of landless households was 17.1% in 1982 and declined to 11.9% in 1992. The percentage of ST landless households increased to 12.8% in 2003, but declined to 9.41% in 2013. 44.82% households of the total estimated households belonged to OBC, owning an estimated 45.68% of the total land in 2013. It is to be noted that this is the highest among all the social groups in terms of households and area owned. Another interesting fact is that only 6.98% of landless households were registered in 2013 in the case of OBC. Thus, Scheduled Caste household's access to land in terms of area of land owned deteriorated during the period 1992 to 2013. It is also to be noted that 50% of ownership holdings of SCs are marginal holdings (0.001–0.40 ha) at the all-India level in 2012–2013, while 25% of holdings of others are marginal holdings (NSSO, 2015, pp. A 204–A208).

3.5 Access to land for SC across the different states in India

It is seen from Table 3.2 that SC rural households constitute 18.87% of total rural households, but they control only 8.60% of total operated area at the all-India level in 2010–2011. Among all the states (union territories) in West Bengal SC households constitute 28.08% of total rural households and control 20.32%of the total operated area, while in Haryana SC households constitute 23.78% of total rural households, but control only 1.19% of the total operated area. It is also noted that in Haryana other constitutes 76.22% of total rural households, but control 98.81% of the total operated area. In the case of Rajasthan, SC households constitute 18.77% (highest) of total rural households and control 17.98% of total operated area. In

Table 3.2 The percentage distribution number of households and operated area among different social groups across the states in India (rural)

	ST		*SC*		*Others*	
States	No.	*Area*	No.	*Area*	No.	*Area*
Andhra Pradesh	8.81	8.73	19.03	7.70	72.16	83.57
Arunachal Pradesh	71.52	99.06	0	0.00	28.48	0.94
Assam	13.04	17.23	7.03	5.05	79.94	77.72
Bihar	1.42	1.65	16.94	9.30	81.64	89.05
Chandigarh	0	0.00	0	0.00	100	100.00
Chhattisgarh	36.89	42.46	13.39	7.80	49.72	49.73
Dadra & Nagar Haveli	75.07	83.25	0.9	0.49	24.02	16.26
Daman & Diu	12.24	9.68	3.58	3.23	84.18	87.10
Delhi	0	0.00	18.85	0.00	81.15	100.00
Goa	14.69	27.08	1.67	0.45	83.64	72.47
Gujarat	22.26	9.78	6.77	2.97	70.97	87.24
Haryana	0	0.00	23.78	1.19	76.22	98.81
Himachal Pradesh	5.81	5.26	25.14	13.82	69.06	80.93
Jammu & Kashmir	15.77	14.50	9.64	8.19	74.59	77.32
Jharkhand	32.54	45.20	12.61	10.17	54.85	44.64
Karnataka	8.78	5.80	19.47	8.83	71.75	85.37
Kerala	2.57	2.28	10.55	2.33	86.88	95.39
Lakshadweep	94.61	82.14	0	0.00	5.39	17.86
Madhya Pradesh	26.19	20.02	16.26	8.46	57.55	71.51
Maharashtra	13.8	7.88	12.69	6.59	73.51	85.52
Manipur	50.36	45.90	2.5	2.50	47.13	51.60
Meghalaya	88.89	99.62	0.55	0.00	10.56	0.38
Mizoram	96.15	99.71	0.05	0.00	3.8	0.29
Nagaland	92.32	99.75	0	0.00	7.68	0.25
Odisha	25.07	33.28	18.03	11.65	56.9	55.07
Puducherry	0	0.00	26.64	3.21	73.36	96.79
Rajasthan	17.7	8.45	18.75	11.67	63.55	79.88
Sikkim	37.63	53.23	4.43	4.69	57.95	42.08
Tamil Nadu	1.72	1.15	24.8	7.59	73.48	91.26
Tripura	39.89	43.49	16.59	14.67	43.52	41.84
Uttar Pradesh	0.66	0.45	24.8	11.18	74.53	88.37
Uttarakhand	3.2	5.87	20.12	8.28	76.67	85.85
West Bengal	7.71	7.20	28.08	20.32	64.21	72.49
India	11.43	11.42	18.87	8.60	69.7	79.99

Source: 1. Census 2011. 2. Agricultural Census, 2010–2011.

the case of Tripura, SC households constitute 16.59% of total rural households and control 14.67% of total operated area. In the case of Kerala, SC households constitute 10.55% of total rural households, but control only 2.33% of the total operating area. In the case of Puducherry, SC households constitute 26.64% of total rural households, but control only 3.21% of total operated area.

In all of the states except Daman & Diu and Sikkim the percentage share of land held by SC households is less than the percentage share of their households in the total rural households. While in case of other, in most states, the share of land is more than the proportionate share of their households in total rural households.

3.6 Access to land for ST across the different states in India

It is also seen from the same table that ST rural households constitute 11.43% of total rural households and control 11.42% of total operated area at the all-India level in 2010–2011.Among all north-eastern states, ST households constitute the highest percentage of total households in Mizoram (96.15%) and control 99.71% of the total operated area. In Nagaland, ST households constitute 92.32% of the total households and control 99.75% of the total operated area. In Meghalaya, ST households constitute 88.89% of total households and control 99.62% of the total operated area, while in Assam ST households constitute only 13.04% of total households and control 17.23% of the total operated area. In plain areas, ST households constitutes the highest percentage in Chhattisgarh (36.89%) of total households and control 42.46% of total operated area, while ST households constitute the lowest percentage (1.42%) of households in Bihar and control 1.65% of total operated area.

3.7 Average size of land holdings

Table 3.3 shows that at the all-India level the average size of operational holding for Scheduled Castes in 2010–2011 was 0.8 hectare. The average size of operational holding in a state is more than 1 hectare for 10 states in 2010–2011.Among the states, Rajasthan occupies first place, where the average size of operational holdings was 2.58 hectares, followed by Punjab (2 hectares) and Gujarat (1.81 hectares). On the other hand, the average size of operational holding is less than 1 hectare for 18 state/UT. This indicates that low access to land for SC despite the land reforms initiated by the various states. The average size of operational holdings was lowest in Kerala (0.07 hectares), followed by Bihar (0.3 hectares) and Tripura (0.36 hectares).

It follows from Table 3.4 that the all-India average size of operational holding for Scheduled Castes in 2010–2011 was 1.52 hectares. Among the states, the average size of operational holding for ST was the highest (6.03 hectares) for Nagaland, followed by Arunachal Pradesh (3.57 hectares), while it was the lowest in Kerala (0.36 hectares), followed by Bihar (0.5 hectares) in 2010–2011. The average size of operational holding for ST was lower than 1 hectare for eight stats/UTs.

Table 3.3 Average size of operational holding for Scheduled Castes

	Agriculture Census 2005–2006						*Agriculture Census 2010–2011*					
States/UTs	*Marginal*	*Small*	*Semi-Medium*	*Medium*	*Large*	*All Size Groups*	*Marginal*	*Small*	*Semi-medium*	*Medium*	*Large*	*All Size Groups*
Andhra Pradesh	0.41	1.38	2.52	5.44	16.49	0.8	0.41	1.38	2.51	5.36	16.5	0.76
Assam	0.46	1.17	2.64	5.13	14.1	0.99	0.42	1.37	2.73	5.17	13.31	1.07
Bihar	0.26	1.24	2.57	4.7	20.93	0.32	0.24	1.26	2.56	5.41	15.88	0.3
Chhattisgarh	0.41	1.39	2.68	5.44	14.28	0.96	0.41	1.38	2.64	5.35	13.9	0.88
Dadra & Nagar Haveli	0.44	1.39	2.47	-	-	0.63	0.4	1.4	2.24	4.16	-	0.57
Daman & Diu	0.24	1.34	2.27	7.43	-	0.37	0.2	1.28	2.56	4.18	-	0.27
Delhi	0.41	-	-	-	-	0.41	0.38	-	-	-	-	0.38
Goa	0.31	1.2	2.2	5.78	20	0.71	0.37	1.77	2.7	6.39	-	0.76
Gujarat	0.51	1.43	2.72	5.69	18.81	1.93	0.48	1.43	2.74	5.79	28.1	1.81
Haryana	0.4	1.44	2.76	5.75	13.92	1.35	0.48	1.48	2.79	5.87	13.04	1.5
Himachal Pradesh	0.38	1.36	2.67	5.48	13.56	0.64	0.38	1.37	2.66	5.46	14.02	0.62
Jammu & Kashmir	0.4	1.38	2.64	5.25	13.35	0.76	0.38	1.4	2.64	5.21	12.06	0.7
Jharkhand	NA	NA	NA	NA	NA	NA	0.42	1.35	2.76	5.42	14.29	0.86
Karnataka	0.49	1.42	2.61	5.54	13.51	1.25	0.48	1.41	2.58	5.48	13.62	1.18
Kerala	0.06	1.32	2.46	5.6	-	0.07	0.06	1.29	2.58	4.73	-	0.07
Madhya Pradesh	0.51	1.38	2.67	5.46	13.89	1.34	0.5	1.36	2.65	5.37	14.1	1.22
Maharashtra	0.46	1.3	2.63	5.64	12.21	1.16	0.48	1.4	2.63	5.53	14.82	1.27
Manipur	0.53	1.07	2.38	4.92	-	1.38	0.54	1.06	2.39	4.83	-	1.37
Odisha	0.47	1.34	2.58	5.25	14.06	0.83	0.52	1.59	2.9	5.79	15.44	0.8
Puducherry	0.35	1.4	2.82	5.4	-	0.65	0.36	1.33	2.63	4.48	-	0.53

Punjab	0.52	1.34	2.51	5.29	13.64	1.6	0.51	1.34	2.51	5.57	13.46	2
Rajasthan	0.52	1.42	2.81	6.09	16.39	2.79	0.51	1.42	2.8	6.07	16.15	2.58
Sikkim	0.42	1.59	2.78	6.66	35.41	1.04	0.36	1.15	2.42	5.3	33.4	1.16
Tamil Nadu	0.35	1.36	2.62	5.42	14.8	0.57	0.35	1.37	2.62	5.45	14.42	0.56
Tripura	0.25	1.35	2.51	5.06	12	0.36	0.25	1.37	2.51	4.81	-	0.36
Uttar Pradesh	0.34	1.35	2.64	5.4	15.28	0.51	0.33	1.35	2.65	5.35	14.9	0.49
Uttarakhand	0.34	1.37	2.59	5.34	22.26	0.54	0.36	1.37	2.58	5.12	17.65	0.54
West Bengal	0.45	1.53	2.68	4.86	-	0.64	0.45	1.56	2.68	4.9	-	0.63
All India	0.37	1.38	2.66	5.72	15.91	0.83	0.37	1.4	2.66	5.7	15.99	0.8

Source: Agricultural Census, 2010–2011.

Table 3.4 Average size of operational holding for Scheduled tribes

	Agriculture Census 2005–2016						*Agriculture Census 2010–2011*					
States	*Marginal*	*Small*	*Semi-medium*	*Medium*	*Large*	*All Size Groups*	*Marginal*	*Small*	*Semi-medium*	*Medium*	*Large*	*All Size Groups*
Andhra Pradesh	0.48	1.41	2.63	5.51	14.33	1.31	0.49	1.4	2.6	5.47	14.53	1.18
Arunachal Pradesh	0.52	1.31	2.79	6.32	13.6	3.31	0.57	1.34	2.76	5.54	14.76	3.57
Assam	0.47	1.23	2.68	5.19	14.43	1.12	0.45	1.39	2.71	5.11	15.33	1.18
Bihar	0.32	1.32	2.62	5.05	16.6	0.52	0.3	1.28	2.55	4.89	13.67	0.5
Chhattisgarh	0.47	1.43	2.69	5.8	17.05	2	0.48	1.43	2.67	5.77	16.86	1.83
Dadra & Nagar Haveli	0.53	1.31	2.71	5.77	14.62	1.35	0.52	1.37	2.75	5.66	13.75	1.31
Daman & Diu	0.27	1.33	2.49	-	-	0.37	0.25	1.37	2.42	9.63	-	0.35
Goa	0.32	1.24	2.51	5.76	16.76	0.67	0.49	1.84	2.92	6	18.42	1.14
Gujarat	0.47	1.44	2.76	5.73	16.68	1.99	0.45	1.44	2.76	5.71	19.49	1.92
Himachal Pradesh	0.42	1.39	2.74	5.38	16.64	0.95	0.41	1.38	2.69	5.37	16.19	0.9
Jammu & Kashmir	0.38	1.4	2.72	5.38	14.31	0.78	0.36	1.41	2.7	5.48	14.81	0.72
Jharkhand	NA	NA	NA	NA	NA	NA	0.45	1.4	2.78	5.71	15.45	1.48
Karnataka	0.51	1.43	2.69	5.7	14.24	1.65	0.5	1.41	2.66	5.59	13.74	1.49
Kerala	0.21	1.31	2.47	4.82	18.89	0.35	0.2	1.32	2.4	5.38	39.27	0.36
Lakshadweep	0.18	1.35	2.45	6.33	10	0.25	0.18	1.35	2.45	6.33	10	0.25
Madhya Pradesh	0.51	1.43	2.71	5.81	13.93	1.99	0.51	1.42	2.68	5.77	13.82	1.78
Maharashtra	0.54	1.31	2.54	5.54	13.9	1.74	0.54	1.43	2.67	5.67	14.65	1.8
Manipur	0.55	1.23	2.44	4.49	-	1.23	0.55	1.23	2.44	4.48	-	1.23
Meghalaya	0.49	1.33	2.54	5.22	13.48	1.17	0.45	1.33	2.79	5.67	14.66	1.37
Mizoram	0.62	1.31	2.32	4.77	13.11	1.19	0.6	1.27	2.42	5.13	15	1.14
Nagaland	0.47	1.17	2.52	6.11	19.46	6.93	0.51	1.13	2.58	6.17	17.57	6.03

Odisha	0.56	1.39	2.67	5.48	13.12	1.24	0.62	1.62	2.92	5.85	16.56	1.13
Rajasthan	0.47	1.41	2.78	5.83	15.73	1.83	0.47	1.41	2.76	5.81	15.87	1.59
Sikkim	0.39	1.31	2.67	5.61	15.63	1.88	0.36	1.21	2.45	5.38	14.55	1.56
Tamil Nadu	0.47	1.39	2.66	5.38	15	1.1	0.45	1.39	2.65	5.43	14.19	1
Tripura	0.36	1.39	2.49	5.24	16.31	0.72	0.35	1.39	2.5	5.05	13.75	0.76
Uttar Pradesh	0.41	1.45	2.74	5.79	15.58	1.26	0.4	1.43	2.76	5.71	15.2	1.13
Uttarakhand	0.36	1.43	2.86	5.86	12.85	1.62	0.36	1.45	2.84	5.79	12.67	1.61
West Bengal	0.48	1.55	2.6	4.89	-	0.72	0.48	1.48	2.64	4.99	-	0.68
All India	0.48	1.39	2.67	5.76	16.32	1.64	0.49	1.43	2.7	5.74	15.95	1.52

Source: Agricultural Census, 2010–2011.

3.8 Occupational distribution of Dalits and general population

Table 3.5 presents the changes in the occupational distribution during 1970–1971 to 2011. It is evident from Table 2.2 that over the period 1971 to 1981 there was an increase in the percentage of SC workers as cultivators from 27.87 to 28.17, while the percentage of SC agricultural labourers declined from 51.75 to 48.22. In the case of general workers the percentage of cultivators declined from 42.9 to 41.58. The percentage of agricultural labourers also declined from 26.9% to 24.94% during the same wperiod. Regarding the non-farming workers, it increased from 20.38% to 23.61% in the case of SC workers. Thus, there is some marginal improvement in the SC workers as cultivators and also as non-farming workers. This indicates some upward mobility of SC workers also. This may be attributed to redistribution of waste lands and surplus lands under the 20 Point Programme in 1970s. But during the period 1981 to 1991 the percentage of SC cultivators declined from 28.17 to 25.44, while there was an increase in the percentage of SC agricultural labourers from 48.22 to 49.06, indicating a downward movement in the case of SC agricultural workers. During the period 1991–2001, there was an increase from 25.44% to 26.78% in the case of cultivators while there was a decline from 49.06% to 46.15% in the case of agricultural labourers. There was an increasing trend in non-farming workers in all categories across all three decades while the increase is significant during the period 1991 to 2011. It should also be noted that the percentage of cultivators declined in all categories, while it is very significant in the case of SCs and STs. During 2001–2011 in the case of the SC main workforce it declined from 26.78% to 14.80% and in case of STs it declined from 54.32% to 34.50%.

Of course, in the case of workers in the general population the percentage of cultivators declined from 41.58 to 38.75, while the percentage of agricultural labourers increased from 24.94 to 26.15 during 1981–1991. Cultivators declined to 31.7%, while the percentage of agricultural labourers remained almost the same during 1991 to 2001. The percentage of cultivators declined further to 24.60 in 2011, while agricultural labourers increased to 30%. However, the percentage of non-farming workers increased from 33.48% to 35.10% in 1991 and further increased to 41.5% and then again to 45.40% in 2011, indicating the occupational shift. In the case of STs, there was a decline in the percentage of cultivators and also in the percentage of agricultural labourers marginally, while there was an increase in the non-agricultural activities from 9.4% in 1971 to 15.8% in 2001. It increased further to 21.00% in 2011.

Thus, during 1971–2011 SC workers mainly remained as agricultural labourers, although there was some change in the composition of agricultural labour. That is, it was revealed from the village-level studies that the percentage of attached labourers declined significantly and converted as casual labourers due to market forces unleashed by the Green Revolution and state intervention in the form of anti-poverty programmes in the

Table 3.5 Occupational distribution at the all-India level

	PERCENTAGE IN TOTAL MAIN WORKERS OF SCs.					*PERCENTAGE IN TOTAL MAIN WORKERS OF STs.*					*PERCENTAGE IN TOTAL MAIN WORKERS OF GENERAL POPULATION*				
CATEGORY	*1971*	*1981*	*1991*	*2001*	*2011*	*1971*	*1981*	*1991*	*2001*	*2011*	*1971*	*1981*	*1991*	*2001*	*2011*
Cultivators	27.87	28.17	25.44	26.78	14.80	55.60	54.43	54.50	54.32	34.50	42.9	41.58	38.75	31.7	24.60
Agricultural labourers	51.75	48.22	49.06	46.15	45.90	33.00	32.67	32.69	29.88	44.50	26.9	24.94	26.15	26.5	30.00
Non-farming workers	20.38	23.61	25.41	27.07	39.30	9.40	12.90	12.81	15.80	21.00	30.2	33.48	35.10	41.5	45.40

Source: 1. Government of India, VII Five Year Plan (1987–1992), Vol. II, p. 330.
2. Census of India, 1991, Series 1, Paper – I, Union Primary Census Abstract for Scheduled Castes/Scheduled Tribes, Census of India 2001.
3. Primary Census Abstract for Total population, Scheduled Castes and Scheduled Tribes, 2011 Office of the Registrar General & Census Commissioner, India.

post-Green Revolution period (Nancharaiah, 1988, pp. 105–106). Many studies on poverty established that poverty has been concentrated among agricultural labour households (Hanumantha Rao. 2005, p. 210).

3.9 Occupational distribution among SCs across the states

It is seen from Table 3.6 that among all the states, in Bihar SC agricultural labour constitutes the highest percentage (69.36%) of the total SC workforce while in Goa SC agricultural labour constitutes the lowest percentage (1.70%) of the total SC workforce. In the case of Andhra Pradesh, SC agricultural labour constitutes 64.36% of the total SC workforce while in Himachal Pradesh, SC agricultural labour constitutes 3.64% of the total SC workforce. In 14 states, SC agricultural labour constitutes more than

Table 3.6 The percentage distribution of Scheduled Caste main workers according to their occupation

States	*Cultivators*	*Agricultural labour*	*Non-farm workers*
Jammu & Kashmir	28.02	7.48	63.03
Himachal Pradesh	50.38	3.64	44.03
Punjab	4.99	31.95	60.01
Uttarakhand	38.75	15.18	43.80
Haryana	5.98	34.14	57.99
NCT of Delhi	0.20	0.95	96.51
Rajasthan	36.37	20.49	41.06
Uttar Pradesh	26.35	37.93	32.10
Bihar	8.57	69.36	19.08
Sikkim	29.35	7.18	60.46
Manipur	41.74	7.74	45.25
Mizoram	3.80	2.81	92.56
Tripura	15.58	18.19	63.88
Meghalaya	7.88	6.81	82.93
Assam	31.20	8.97	55.08
West Bengal	17.09	35.17	43.09
Jharkhand	15.15	29.68	50.35
Odisha	21.08	33.25	41.06
Chhattisgarh	25.92	39.84	32.63
Madhya Pradesh	19.89	42.70	32.87
Gujarat	8.27	34.67	55.62
Daman & Diu	1.46	0.45	97.58
Dadra & Nagar Haveli	4.55	1.76	93.16
Maharashtra	10.58	44.60	42.70
Andhra Pradesh	7.95	64.36	26.30
Karnataka	18.13	38.16	41.59
Goa	3.33	1.70	92.70
Kerala	1.64	21.22	75.85
Tamil Nadu	7.59	46.99	43.73
Puducherry	1.62	33.08	64.35

Source: Census 2011.

30% in each state. Thus, in the case of Andhra, for example, 72.31% of the total SC workforce depends on agriculture for their livelihood. In the case of cultivators, Himachal Pradesh occupies first place where cultivators constitute 50.38% while in the case of Kerala cultivators constitute the lowest percentage (1.64) of total SC workforce. In ten states, SC cultivators constitute less than 20% of the total SC workforce. Regarding the non-farming SC workers, among the states, Delhi occupies first place, where non-farm workers constitute 96.51% of the SC total workforce, while it is only 19.08% in the case of Bihar. More than 50% of states/UTs, SC non-farm workers constitute 50% of the total workforce in each state as per the 2011 population census.

3.10 Occupational distribution among STs across the states

It follows from Table 3.7 that among all the states, ST agricultural labour constitutes the highest percentage (64.99) of the total ST workforce in Bihar, followed by Maharashtra (54.92) and Andhra Pradesh (52.76), while ST agricultural labour constitutes the lowest percentage (2.95) in Arunachal Pradesh, followed by Nagaland (2.53) and Himachal Pradesh (2.95). In the case of cultivators, among the north-eastern states, Manipur occupies first place, with cultivators constituting 73.37% of the total workforce, followed by Arunachal Pradesh (68.17%) and Assam (65.87%). In the case of other states, Rajasthan occupies first place, with cultivators constituting 65.29% of the total workforce, followed by Uttarkhand (57.66%) and Chhattisgarh (52.74%).

It also noted that in the case of Andhra Pradesh, 82.46% of the total ST workforce depends on agriculture as either cultivators (29.70%) or agricultural labourers (52.76%). Among the states, ST non-farming workers constitutes the highest percentage (72.47) of total ST workers in Goa, followed by Jammu and Kashmir (48.56) and Kerala (48.27), while it is at its lowest in Madhya Pradesh (12.48%), followed by Bihar (14.53) and Andhra Pradesh (15.74) (Table 3.8)

3.11 Micro studies

An attempt is also made with the help of some micro studies relating to land transfers with special reference to Dalits to understand the process of change the distribution of land of Dalits in terms of their access to land at macro level.

Nageswara Rao, in his study entitled "Green Revolution and Land Transfers: A Case Study of a Village in Coastal Andhra" (Nageswara Rao, 1988, pp. 85–89), analysed the land transfers among different caste groups with special reference to Dalits in the post-Independence Period during 1960–1961 to 1996–1997. He has selected a village, namely 'Poondla' in Guntur District of Andhra Pradesh. From this village, out of a total of 1135

Table 3.7 The percentage distribution of Scheduled Tribes main workers according to their occupation

States	*Cultivators*	*Agricultural labour*	*Non-farm workers*
Jammu & Kashmir	40.47	9.18	48.56
Himachal Pradesh	49.88	2.95	45.22
Uttarakhand	57.66	14.00	24.99
Rajasthan	65.29	14.32	19.88
Uttar Pradesh	26.84	39.89	29.78
Bihar	18.28	64.99	14.53
Sikkim	44.13	6.18	48.64
Arunachal Pradesh	68.17	2.11	28.87
Nagaland	64.72	2.53	31.50
Manipur	73.37	3.24	21.64
Mizoram	51.33	6.35	41.07
Tripura	40.00	28.86	30.14
Meghalaya	49.96	13.41	35.33
Assam	65.87	8.10	23.56
West Bengal	15.35	49.39	33.49
Jharkhand	49.15	22.53	25.96
Odisha	40.45	32.55	24.42
Chhattisgarh	52.74	31.52	14.79
Madhya Pradesh	41.46	45.38	12.48
Gujarat	34.23	44.74	20.33
Daman & Diu	2.38	2.43	94.65
Dadra & Nagar Haveli	41.40	11.13	46.24
Maharashtra	26.41	54.92	17.77
Andhra Pradesh	29.70	52.76	15.74
Karnataka	28.97	38.30	30.63
Goa	17.55	8.18	72.47
Lakshadweep	0.00	0.00	99.01
Kerala	10.09	40.59	48.27
Tamil Nadu	29.93	41.11	27.46
Andaman & Nicobar Islands	1.30	0.51	87.98

Source: Census 2011.

households, he selected a sample of 141 households for intensive study. The study finds the following:

a) The SC landless households, which constituted 20% of total SC households in 1980–1981, increased to 27% in 1991 and increased further to about 55% by 1996–1997. In every decade, the landless households among SCs was doubled during 1960–1961 to 1996–1997, while the number of landless households among others declined during the same period. The landless households, among others, declined from 30% of total households of others to 16%. The main reasons for the increase in the landless households among SCs are found to be that land transfers took place consistent with Caste hierarchy and the failure of land reforms in addition to the population explosion.

Table 3.8 The percentage distribution of the general population of main workers, according to their occupation

State/UTs	*Cultivators*	*Agricultural labour*	*Non-farmworkers*
Jammu & Kashmir	21.42	6.03	72.54
Himachal Pradesh	44.60	3.33	52.07
Punjab	21.35	13.82	64.83
Chandigarh	0.56	0.36	99.08
Uttarakhand	36.43	8.61	54.96
Haryana	27.99	12.70	59.31
NCT of Delhi	0.52	0.59	98.88
Rajasthan	46.75	10.43	42.82
Uttar Pradesh	34.90	21.84	43.26
Bihar	25.34	44.65	30.01
Sikkim	35.90	5.03	59.08
Arunachal Pradesh	51.83	4.23	43.94
Nagaland	56.72	3.05	40.24
Manipur	42.77	5.12	52.11
Mizoram	48.80	6.38	44.83
Tripura	22.91	18.74	58.35
Meghalaya	44.63	12.44	42.93
Assam	36.13	10.40	53.47
West Bengal	16.37	22.85	60.78
Jharkhand	29.35	18.17	52.48
Odisha	30.63	22.61	46.76
Chhattisgarh	36.86	30.41	32.73
Madhya Pradesh	36.19	29.21	34.61
Gujarat	23.31	22.06	54.64
Daman & Diu	1.42	0.42	98.16
Dadra & Nagar Haveli	17.43	4.75	77.83
Maharashtra	26.23	25.29	48.48
Andhra Pradesh	18.43	39.96	41.61
Karnataka	25.81	21.88	52.31
Goa	5.05	2.26	92.69
Lakshadweep	0.00	0.00	100.00
Kerala	5.84	9.85	84.31
Tamil Nadu	13.80	25.89	60.31
Puducherry	2.69	12.66	84.65
Andaman &Nicobar Islands	10.32	2.13	87.55
India	26.44	23.77	49.78

Source: Census 2011.

b) In the post-Green Revolution period, the land has been transferred from dominant non-cultivating castes to dominant cultivating castes and BCs, but not to the SC/STs who were the actual tillers. And the marginal and small holders have leased-out and some of them sold away their lands to the medium and large farmers. In the first two decades, 1960–1961 to 1980–1981, the land has transferred from Dominant Non-cultivating Costs (DNCCs) to Dominant Cultivating

> Costs (DCCs). The DCCS had gained 21% and 25% of the total land transfers, respectively, during these decades. In the second two decades, 1980–1981 to 1990–1991 and 1990–1991 to 1996–1997, the land has transferred from DNCCs and DCCs to BCs. BCs had gained 28% and 27% of the total land transfers, respectively, in the third decade and after 1990–1991, while the SCs had gained during 1960–1961 to 1996–1997, only 4% of the total land transferred, although they were the actual tillers of the lands of DNCCs and DCCs.

In his case study of a village in Alur Taluk of Kurnool district of Rayalaseema region of Rajasekhar (Rajasekhar, 1988, pp. 1–78) studied the transfers which occurred during the period 1891–1994. The study finds that in the period 1891–1948, Brahmins lost their land of 907 acres and other upper castes Reddies had gained 915 acres out of the total land transferred. In the post-Independence period, that is, during 1948–1984, Upper Caste Brahmins and others lost 86% and Muslims lost 14% of the total land transfers. By contrast, Yadavas (OBCs) gained 48% and Valmikis gained 36.24% to the total land transfers. SCs gained only 15% and Artisans got only 6% of the total land transfers in the village.

Venkat, in his study of Dsantapalli, Utnoor Taluk in Adilabad district of Telangana region of Andhra Pradesh (a Scheduled Village) on the basis of primary data, pertaining to 1960–1961 to 1990–1991 (Venkati 1994, pp. 316–331) finds the following:

In every decade Komatis [the dominant non-cultivating community] lost their land due to non-interest in agriculture and fear of land legislation. Kapus, the dominant cultivating caste, gained 30% during 1960–1961 to 1970–1971, 29% during 1970–1971 to 1980–1981 of the total land transfers as major shares. In the second phase, Kumbis gained 16% of the total land transfers. Similarly, Gowdas gained 28% of the total land transfers during the decade from 1980–1981 to 1990–1991. In the first decade, the major share of land transferred from Komaties, SCs & STs to Kapus. During the second and third decades, major shares of land transferred from SCs & STs and Kapus to Gowdas & Kumbis, the next dominant caste in the hierarchy.

Thus, Kapus (upper castes) Gowdas and Kumbis (upper BCs) while Komatis (OCs) and SCs & STs were the losers during the period of 1960–1961 to 1990–1991 in the village.

Kripa Shankar, in his study of land transfers in Utter Pradesh since the abolition of Zamindary, shows that a significant proportion of the land passed from Zamindars into the hands of large landowners who belonged to the upper caste (Sagar, 1988, pp. 1514–1517). The study is confined to only such transfers which were duly registered with the government and covers the post-Zamindari abolition period of about 30 years in the selected 19 districts of the State: 7 from Eastern Uttar Pradesh, 5 from Central Uttar Pradesh, 5 from Western Utter Pradesh and 1 each from Bundelkhand and the hill region. The total number of land transfers studied were 1730 for the state. The main findings of the study are as follows:

The upper caste landholders lost their land as a result of the Land Tenancy Act, and they were non-cultivating communities. They lost 18% of the total land transfers, while the other Backward Castes landholders gained 16% of the total land transfers as a major share. Scheduled Castes and Sikhs made marginal gains, of only about 2% and 1% of the total land transfers respectively, during the same period.

Nancharaiah, in his study on "Land and Caste", examined the change in the direction and magnitude of shifts in land distribution among different caste groups during 1930 to 1982 on the basis of the data collected from land records and household surveys (Nancharaiah, 1988, pp. 80–86). An inamdari village, namely Kanchakoduru of Krishna District in Andhra Pradesh, was selected for this study. This study clearly shows that in 1930 more than nearly 80% of the total land under the revenue jurisdiction of the village was controlled by Brahmins who were inamdars. Non-Brahmin Castes who were landless agricultural labourers controlled only about 1% of the total land area in 1930. However, by 1965 there was a significant shift in the land distribution pattern in the context of land legislation initiated by the government. About 80% of the total land was under the control of non-Brahmin cultivating castes (Kapus, an advanced caste) and the SCs' share improved slightly to about 15%, while the Brahmins' share declined to about 7% in the total amount of land. By 1982, there was a further shift in the pattern of land distribution and more than 85% of the total land of the village came under the control of non-Brahmin castes while the share of Brahmins (non-cultivating advanced castes) declined further, to only 3%. And the share of SCs also declined from 15% to 10% during the period 1965–1982 while their population constitutes 38% of the total population. It is also to be noted that this period from 1965 onwards was the post-Green Revolution period, where there is a decline in the number of marginal holdings and the area under their control. Thus, this study also shows clearly that neither the benefits of land legislation nor the benefits of the Green Revolution reached the Scheduled Castes in terms of their access to land.

Thus, the findings of the above analysed five microstudies confirm that the land has passed into the hands of dominant cultivating castes and upper BCs consistent with caste hierarchy. In this process of land transfers in the post-Independence period, it is also found from these studies that Dalits could not gain; as a result, they essentially remained as agricultural labourers as they were in the pre-Independence period and furthermore the position of SCs deteriorated in terms of land ownership in the post-Green Revolution period at the micro level as SC farmers were mostly marginal farmers consistent with macro-level evidence. This may be the reason why there is evidence of an increase in the percentage of landless households of SCs in rural India.

3.12 Incidence of poverty among Dalits

The data on incidence of poverty among various social groups at the all-India level are presented in Table 3.9.

It is evident from the Table 3.9 that the incidence of poverty has declined during 1993–1994 to 2009–2010 in all social groups. But the incidence of poverty among SCs and STs was much higher than the incidence of poverty among all social groups in 2009–2010. The incidence of poverty among STs has declined from 65.7% in 1993–1994 to 64.5% in 2004--2005 and that it declined further, to 47.4% in 2009–10 in rural areas, while it has declined from 40.9% to 38.7% and declined further to 30.4% during the same period in urban areas. In the case of SCs also, it has declined from 62.1% in 1993–1994 to 53.6% in 2004–2005, and declined further to 42.3% in 2009–2010 in rural areas, while it has declined from 51.4% to 40.6% and further declined to 34.1% during the same period in urban areas. In the case of OBCs the incidence of poverty declined from 39.8% in 2004–2005 to 31.9% in 2009–2010 in rural areas, while it has declined

Table 3.9 National rural and urban poverty lines by social groups based on the Tendulkar line

	Rural		
Social groups	*1993–1994*	*2004–2005*	*2009–2010*
ST	65.7	64.5	47.4
SC	62.1	53.6	42.3
OBC	43.8	39.8	31.9
FC		27.1	21.0
NS		35.1	28.0
ALL	50.1	41.8	33.3
		Urban	
ST	40.9	38.7	30.4
SC	51.4	40.6	34.1
OBC	28.1	30.8	24.3
FC		16.2	12.4
NS		22.6	18.0
ALL	31.7	25.8	20.9
		R+U	
ST	63.5	62.4	45.6
SC	60.2	51.0	40.6
OBC	39.5	37.9	30.0
FC		23.0	17.6
NS		31.5	24.9
ALL	45.5	37.9	29.9

Note: FC = forward castes, NS = non-scheduled, OBC = other backward castes, SC = Scheduled Castes, ST = Scheduled Tribes.

Source: Arvind Panagriya And Megha Mukim (2014), "A Comprehensive Analysis of Poverty in India", *Asian Development Review*, Vol. 31, No. 1 p. 15.

from 30.8% to 24.3% in urban areas during the same period. In the case of FCs the incidence of poverty declined from 27.1% in 2004–2005 to 21.0% in 2009–2010 in rural areas, while it has declined from 16.2% to 12.4% in urban areas during the same period. In the case of NS (Non-scheduled) also the incidence of poverty has declined from 35.1% in 2004–2005 to 28.0% in 2009–2010 in rural areas, while it has declined from 22.6% to 18.0% in urban areas during the same period. In the case of all groups the incidence of poverty has declined from 50.1% in 1993–1994 to 41.9% in 2004–2005 and then declined further to 33.3% in 2009–2010 in rural areas, while it has declined from 31.7% to 25.8% and further declined to 20.9% during the same period in urban areas.

The overall incidence of poverty (rural + urban) has declined from 63.5% in 1993–1994 to 62.4% in 2004–2005 and declined further to 45.6% in 2009–2010 in the case of STs, while it has declined from 60.2% to 51.0% in 2004–2005 and further declined to 40.6% during the same period in the case of SCs. In the case of OBCs also the overall (rural + urban) incidence of poverty has declined from 37.9%in 2004–2005 to 30% in 2009–2010. In the case of FCs, the overall (rural + urban) incidence of poverty has declined from 23.0% in 2004–2005 to 17.6% in 2009–2010. In the case of all groups, it has declined from 45.5% in 1993–1994 to 37.9% in 2004–2005 and further declined to 29.9% in 2009–2010. In the case of NS the incidence of overall (rural + urban) poverty has declined from 31.5% in 2004–2005 to 24.9% in 2009–2010. It is also observed that the overall incidence of poverty (rural + urban) among SCs and STs is much higher than the incidence of poverty in all social groups. Thus, in the post-liberalisation period the incidence of poverty has declined among all social groups, but it is still higher in case of STs/SCs at the all-India level in 2009–2010.

One important reason for the high incidence of poverty among Dalits, particularly Scheduled Castes, is the high incidence of landlessness and their heavy dependence on agriculture as agricultural labourers. This is because of the failure of the land reform in Indian agriculture in reducing the inequalities in the distribution of land. Of course, land reform was successful to the extent of abolishing intermediary land tenures and reducing the incidence of tenancy. But it did not benefit agricultural labourers and other weaker sections. Land passed into the hands of dominant peasant communities (owner-cultivator class) form old Jamindars (rentier class) but land concentration persists.

It is observed from Table 3.10 that the incidence of poverty among all the social groups (ST, SC and NS) has declined in all of the 17 states during the period 1993–1994 to 2009–2010, with the exception of Chhattisgarh, where the incidence of poverty has increased marginally in the case of SCs and STs. In the case of STs, the incidence of poverty has increased during 1993–1994 to 2004–2005 and declined during 2004–205 to 2009–2010 in six states: Maharashtra, Andhra Pradesh, Madhya Pradesh, Gujarat, Orissa and Kerala. In the case of SCs the incidence of poverty has also increased during 1993–1994 to 2004–2005 and declined during 2004–2005 to

Table 3.10 Poverty in the states by social groups based on the Tendulkar Line (%)

States	*ST*			*SC*			*NS*		
	1993–1994	*2004–2005*	*2009–2010*	*1993-1994*	*2004-2005*	*2009–2010*	*1993–1994*	*2004–2005*	*2009–2010*
Uttar Pradesh	45.7	41.7	40.1	68.1	55.2	52.4	42.8	36.7	32.9
Maharashtra	71.5	68.1	48.5	65	52.9	34.7	41.9	32.3	19.8
Bihar	72.1	59.1	62	75.4	77	67.7	56	48.2	49.2
Andhra Pradesh	56.7	59.3	37.6	61.7	40.3	24.5	39.8	24.7	19.4
West Bengal	64.2	54	31.6	48.5	37.9	32.6	33.5	31.9	24.5
Tamil Nadu	47.4	41.9	14.1	64	48.6	28.8	39.4	25.5	14.7
Madhya Pradesh	68.3	77.4	61	55.6	62	41.9	33	35.9	27.9
Rajasthan	62.1	57.9	35.4	54	49	37.1	29.6	25.2	18.7
Gujarat	51.2	54.7	47.6	54.1	40.1	21.8	32.6	27.1	17.6
Karnataka	68.6	51.2	24.2	69.1	53.8	34.4	43.6	27.6	21.2
Orissa	80.4	82.8	62.7	60.6	67.4	47.1	50.6	44.8	24
Kerala	35.2	54.4	21.2	50.3	31.2	27.4	29.4	17.8	10.4
Assam	54.1	28.8	31.9	57.8	44.3	36.6	51.3	35.2	40.2
Jharkhand	71.2	59.8	50.9	72.5	59.7	43.5	53.3	38.9	31.5
Haryana	65.7	6.7	57.4	59.1	47.4	37.8	27.4	16.3	12.1
Punjab	36.8	18.7	15.5	37.7	37.9	29.2	13.9	11.5	7.3
Chhattisgarh	64	62.9	65	52.6	48	60.1	42.1	44.5	39.6
Total	63.5	62.4	45.6	60.2	51	40.6	39.3	31.5	24.9

Note: FC = forward castes, NS = non-scheduled, OBC = other backward castes, SC = Scheduled Castes, ST = Scheduled Tribes.

Source: Arvind Panagriya And Megha Mukim (2014) "A Comprehensive Analysis of Poverty in India", *Asian Development Review*, Vol. 31, No. 1, p. 27.

2009–2010 in three states: Bihar, Madhya Pradesh and Orissa. The incidence of poverty among STs is highest in Chhattisgarh, standing at 65% even in 2009–2010. The incidence of poverty is above 60% in three states: Orissa (62.7), Bihar (62) and Madhya Pradesh (61) in 2009–2010.The incidence of poverty is above 50% in two states: Jharkhand (50.9) and Haryana (57.4) in 2009–2010. The incidence of poverty among STs is lowest in Tamil Nadu (14.1), followed by Punjab (15.5) in 2009–2010. The incidence of poverty among STs is below 20% in two states: Kerala (21.2) and Karnataka (24.2).

In the case of SCs, the incidence of poverty is highest in Bihar (67.7), followed by Chhattisgarh (60.1) and Uttar Pradesh (52.4) in 2009–2010. The incidence of poverty is lowest in Gujarat (21.8), followed by Andhra Pradesh (24.5) in 2009–2010 and the incidence of poverty was less than 30% in three more states: Kerala (27.4), Tamil Nadu (28.8) and Punjab (29.2). It is also observed that in all of the 17 states the incidence of poverty in the case of SCs and STs was higher than the incidence of poverty among non-scheduled castes in 2009–2010, with the exception of two states: Tamil Nadu (where the incidence of poverty in STs is lower than that of NS) and Assam.

Thus, in the post-liberalisation period the incidence of poverty has declined among all the social groups, but it is still higher in case of STs and SCs in 2009–2010.

It can be seen from Table 3.11 that the incidence of poverty among all social groups (ST, SC and others) has declined in all of the 20 states during the period 1993–1994 to 2009–2010, except for Chhattisgarh, where the incidence of poverty has increased marginally in the case of SCs and STs in rural areas. The incidence of poverty among STs is highest in Chhattisgarh (66.8%), even in 2009–2010 in rural areas. The incidence of poverty is above 60% in three other states: Orissa (66), Bihar (64.4) and Madhya Pradesh (61.9) in 2009–2010 in rural areas. The incidence of poverty is above 50% in only one state – Maharashtra (51.7) – in 2009–2010 in rural areas. The incidence of poverty among STs is lowest in Tamil Nadu (11.5%), followed by Punjab (16.1%) in 2009–2010 in rural areas.

In the case of SCs, the incidence of poverty is highest in Bihar (68.1%), followed by Chhattisgarh (67.6%) and Uttar Pradesh (53.6%) in 2009–2010 in rural areas. The incidence of poverty is lowest in Himachal Pradesh (14.4%), followed by Gujarat (17.9%) in 2009–2010 in rural areas. It is also observed that in all 20 states the incidence of poverty in the case of SCs and STs was higher than the incidence of poverty among others in 2009–2010 in rural areas, with the exception of Assam. Thus, in the post-liberalisation period the incidence of poverty has declined among all the social groups, but it is still higher in the case of STs and SCs in 2009–2010 in rural areas.

It is observed from above Table 3.12 that the incidence of poverty has declined during the period 1993–1994 to 2009–2010 in the case of STs in 13 states out of 20 states in urban areas, while in the case of SCs it has declined in all the states except Haryana and Orissa during the same period.

Table 3.11 Rural poverty by state and by social group based on the Tendulkar line using MRP expenditures: Scheduled Castes, Scheduled Tribes, and all groups (%)

	ST			*SC*			*Others*		
States	*1993–1994*	*2004–2005*	*2009–2010*	*1993–1994*	*2004–2005*	*2009–2010*	*1993–1994*	*2004–2005*	*2009–2010*
Andhra Pradesh	58.1	60.3	40.2	64.2	41.8	25.7	48	32.3	22.7
Assam	55.3	28.8	32	58.4	45.3	36.9	55	36.3	39.9
Bihar	73.3	59.3	64.4	76	77.6	68.1	62.3	55.7	55.2
Chhattisgarh	65.9	65.5	66.8	53.4	48.6	67.6	55.9	55.1	56.1
Delhi	0	-	0	27.9	0	0	16.2	15.6	7.6
Gujarat	53.1	57.1	48.6	56.3	49.3	17.9	43.1	39.1	26.6
Haryana	69.7	0	49.6	63.1	47.5	33.6	39.9	24.8	18.6
Himachal Pradesh	62.4	35.4	22	43.6	39.4	14.4	36.7	25	9.1
Jharkhand	72.6	60.6	51	73.7	61	44.1	65.7	51.6	41.4
Karnataka	70.3	50.5	21.3	72.4	57.4	35.6	56.4	37.4	26.2
Kerala	40.9	56.9	24.4	53.3	30.8	27.7	33.8	20.2	12
Madhya Pradesh	69.8	80	61.9	59.3	62.5	42.4	48.8	53.6	42
Maharashtra	74.2	73.2	51.7	73.8	66.1	37.6	59.2	47.8	29.5
Orissa	82.1	84.4	66	62.8	67.9	47.1	63	60.7	39.2
Punjab	35.9	30.7	16.1	34.6	38.4	27.2	20.1	22.1	14.6
Rajasthan	63.7	59.3	35.9	55.3	48.5	38.6	40.7	35.9	26.4
Tamil Nadu	57	47.3	11.5	66.3	51.2	31.2	51	37.6	21.2
Uttar Pradesh	49.6	42	49.8	68.6	56.6	53.6	50.9	42.7	39.4
Uttarakhand	54.9	32.4	20	43.5	46.2	20	36.7	35.1	13.7
West Bengal	66.5	54.3	32.9	48.2	37.1	31.5	42.4	38.3	28.8
Total	65.7	64.5	47.4	62.1	53.6	42.3	50.1	41.9	33.3

Note: MRP = mixed reference period, SC = Scheduled Castes, ST = Scheduled Tribes.

Source: Arvind Panagriya And Megha Mukim (2014) "A Comprehensive Analysis of Poverty in India", *Asian Development Review*, Vol. 31, No. 1, p. 45.

Table 3.12 Urban poverty by state and by social groups based on the Tendulkar line using MRP expenditures: Scheduled Castes, Scheduled Tribes, and all groups (%)

	ST			*SC*			*Others*		
States	*1993–1994*	*2004–2005*	*2009–2010*	*1993–1994*	*2004–2005*	*2009–2010*	*1993–1994*	*2004–2005*	*2009–2010*
Andhra Pradesh	43.9	50.1	21.2	45.6	35	19.8	35.1	23.4	17.7
Assam	17	29.8	29.2	49.7	37.2	34.9	27.7	21.8	25.9
Bihar	43.1	57.2	16.5	66.5	71.2	61	44.6	43.7	39.4
Chhattisgarh	18.6	32.7	28.6	48.5	44.6	29.7	28.1	28.4	23.6
Delhi	9.1	0	67.9	48.8	26.2	33.7	15.7	12.9	14.3
Gujarat	31	31.2	32.2	49.3	18.7	29.4	28	20.1	17.6
Haryana	0	22.2	85	41.8	46.9	48.3	24.2	22.4	23
Himachal Pradesh	0	2.4	19.6	26.9	9.2	20.4	13.6	4.6	12.5
Jharkhand	56.1	47.2	49.5	67.9	52.6	40.5	41.8	23.8	31
Karnataka	56.9	55.7	35.6	55.4	41.2	29.5	34.2	25.9	19.5
Kerala	0	21.8	5	34.7	33	25.8	23.7	18.4	12.1
Madhya Pradesh	51.2	42.6	41.6	45.1	59.6	39.2	31.7	35.1	22.8
Maharashtra	56.1	34.8	32.4	48.2	36	30.4	30.2	25.6	18.3
Orissa	56.5	53.4	34.1	39	63.7	47.1	34.3	37.6	25.9
Punjab	42.1	2.4	15	50.6	36.2	35.3	27.2	18.7	18
Rajasthan	12.6	26.8	28.9	49.1	51	31.6	29.9	29.7	19.9
Tamil Nadu	25.4	34.7	17.6	56.5	40.7	23.4	33.5	19.8	12.7
Uttar Pradesh	27.9	40.3	20.2	63.8	44.2	42.2	38.2	34.1	31.7
Uttaranchal	-	39	0	0	47.5	28.1	18.7	26.2	25
West Bengal	28.1	48	20.6	50.1	40.9	38.2	31.2	24.4	21.9
Total	40.9	38.7	30.4	51.4	40.6	34.1	31.7	25.8	20.9

Note: MRP = Mixed Reference Period, SC = Scheduled Castes, ST = Scheduled Tribes.

Source: Arvind Panagriya And Megha Mukim (2014), "A Comprehensive Analysis of Poverty in India", *Asian Development Review*, Vol. 31, No. 1 p. 47.

In the case of others, the incidence of poverty declined during 1993–1994 to 2009–2010 in all the states (with the exception of Uttaranchal) in urban areas. The incidence of poverty is above 60% in two states – Haryana (85) and Delhi (67.9) – in 2009–2010 in urban areas. The incidence of poverty among STs is lowest in Kerala (5%), followed by Punjab (15%) and Bihar (16.5%) in 2009–2010 in urban areas.

In the case of SCs the incidence of poverty is highest in Bihar (61%), followed by Haryana (48.3%) in 2009–2010 in urban areas. The incidence of poverty is lowest in Andhra Pradesh (19.8%), followed by Himachal Pradesh (20.4%) in 2009–2010 in urban areas. The incidence of poverty among SCs/STs was higher than the incidence of poverty in others in all states, except Bihar, Kerala, Punjab and Uttar Pradesh (where the incidence of poverty in the case of STs is lower than that of other in 2009–2010).

3.13 Consumption pattern among social groups

From Table 3.13 it follows that there has been an increase in the per capita consumer expenditure by all social groups in rural areas at the all-India level during the period 1983–1984 to 1987–1988. It is also noted that agriculture registered a higher growth rate of 3.2% during the 1980s. However, there was a significant gap between per capita consumption expenditure of SCs/STs and others. The per capita consumption expenditure of SCs was 78.3% of that of others and consumption of STs was 72.4% of that of others in 1983–1984 and the gap remained almost same in 1987–1988 despite a significant increase in the agricultural growth rate during the same period. It is also to be noted from the table that the per capita consumption expenditure per 30 days of SCs/STs was better in agriculturally advanced states like Punjab and Haryana than in agriculturally backward states like Bihar and Madhya Pradesh. However, the gap between the per capita consumption expenditure of SCs/STs and others was larger in advanced states like Punjab and Haryana than in agriculturally backward states like Bihar and Madhya Pradesh. In 1983–1984, the per capita consumption of SCs in Punjab was 70.9% of that of others in 1983–1984 and 65.4% in 1987–1988 while it was 76.4% in 1983–1984 and 80.7% in Bihar. In Haryana, the per capita consumption of SCs was 70.9% of that of others in 1983–1984 and 70% in 1987–1988, while in Madhya Pradesh it was 73.5% in 1983–1984 and 78.3% in 1987–1988; that is, the gap is not only higher in technologically advanced states than in technologically backward states, but the gap has been widening. It clearly indicates that the benefits of agricultural growth resulting from new technology largely benefited the upper strata; the lower strata did not get any significant benefit as they happened to be mostly agricultural labourers.

There has been an increasing per capita consumer expenditure of all social groups in rural areas at the all-India level during the period 1987–1988 to 2009–2010. However, there is a significant gap between the per capita consumer expenditure of SC/STs and others. The per capita consumption

Table 3.13 Average monthly per capita consumer expenditure by social groups state-wise in rural India

States	*ST*			*SC*			*OBC*			*Others*			*All households*		
	83–84	*87–88*	*2009–2010*	*83–84*	*87–88*	*2009–2010*	*83–84*	*87–88*	*2009–2010*	*83–84*	*87–88*	*2009–2010*	*83–84*	*87–88*	*2009–2010*
Andhra Pradesh	94.29	120.79	999	97.84	132.32	1155	-	-	1184	121.83	169.06	1571			1234
Arunachal Pradesh	202.12	-	1589			1330	-	-	951			1503			1546
Assam	108.80	145.12	1032	111.07	166.00	992	-	-	1100	114.17	160.80	933			1003
Bihar	80.68	122.98	848	76.02	114.54	697	-	-	759	99.49	141.96	927			780
Chhattisgarh	-	-	747			709	-	-	831			904			784
Delhi	-			22.85		1417	-	-	2345			3060			2068
Goa	-	-	1854	-			-	-	1467			2296			2065
Gujarat	87.50	131.73	879	103.47	144.01	1088	-	-	1038	131.04	172.52	1590			1110
Haryana	-	195.20	1401	113.64	168.24	1165	-	-	1375	160.39	239.88	1835			1510
Himachal Pradesh	-	212.13	1370	125.69	179.93	1350	-	-	1396	159.70	217.00	1679			1536
Jammu & Kashmir	-	176.58	1223	112.96	179.93	1186	-	-	1266	129.79	198.96	1392			1344
Jharkhand	-	-	775			780	-	-	852			971			825
Karnataka	87.84	130.48	901	94.61	112.07	934	-	-	1021	125.14	159.45	1121			1020
Kerala	-	186.69	1208	105.07	163.39	1400	-	-	1706	150.74	215.53	2295			1835
Madhya Pradesh	79.43	106.49	681	87.47	124.98	839	-	-	969	119.02	159.66	1269			903
Maharashtra	90.01	129.78	961	93.60	130.80	1031	-	-	1135	116.75	168.36	1309			1153
Manipur	122.28	167.58	1012	-	-	1196	-	-	1038	137.97	192.66	987			1027
Meghalaya	-	167.51	1116	-	202.15	1632	-	-	765	-	192.10	1123			1110
Mizoram	-	-	1266	-	216.30	963	-	-	997	-		1606			1262

(*Continued*)

Table 3.13 (Continued)

	ST			*SC*			*OBC*			*Others*			*All households*		
States	*83–84*	*87–88*	*2009–2010*	*83–84*	*87–88*	*2009–2010*	*83–84*	*87–88*	*2009–2010*	*83–84*	*87–88*	*2009–2010*	*83–84*	*87–88*	*2009–2010*
Nagaland	72.73	-	1477	-	--	1198	-	-	1335	-		1522			1476
Odisha	-	93.72	629	87.30	117.63	757	-	-	862	110.63		1018			818
Punjab	90.11	-	1510	132.05	178.91	1271	-	-	1723	186.30		2069			1649
Rajasthan	-	125.26	984	110.17	160.01	986	-	-	1289	140.01		1316			1179
Sikkim	-	152.82	1249	-	145.57	1362	-	-	1311	-		1843			1321
Tamil Nadu	-	151.95	989	87.53	118.13	1003	-	-	1220	119.74		1350			1160
Tripura	-	155.01	1053	-	158.55	1179	-	-	1176	-		1376			1176
Uttar Pradesh	-	132.90	873	88.57	124.72	804	-	-	880	108.82		1086			899
Uttarakhand	-	-	1016	-	-	1064	-	-	1410	-		2106			1747
West Bengal	85.29	127.18	875	94.99	137.28	897	-	-	951	110.95		992			952
Andaman & Nicobar Islands	146.07	252.44	1825	151.45	-	4162	-	-	2232	159.56		1870			1932
Chandigarh	-	131.73		116.60	-	1724	-	-	3192	220.77		2392			2227
Dadra N. Haveli	82.36	111.73	854	-	-	2275	-	-	962	179.81		1418			915
Daman & Diu	124.12	159.94	885	-	-	2157	-	-	1564	172.37		2109			1586
Lakshadweep	-	232.21	1793	-	-	2089	-	-	1621	-					1794
Puducherry	-	-		69.80	127.24	1361	-	-	1698	109.62		2270			1636
All India	87.15	123.04	873	94.31	133.36	929	-	-	1036	120.42		1281			1054

Source: NSSO Report No. 544 (66th round, July 2009–June 2010).

expenditure of SCs was 72.52% of that of others and the consumption of STs was 68.14% of that of others in 2009–2010 at the all-India level. It is also to be noted from Table 2.4 that the per capita consumption expenditure of SC/STs was better in agriculturally advanced states like Punjab and Haryana than in agriculturally backward states like Bihar and Madhya Pradesh. However, the gap between the per capita consumption expenditure of SC/STs and others was larger in advanced states like Punjab and Haryana than in the backward state like Bihar.

3.14 Conclusion

Dalits, particularly SCs, mostly remained as agricultural labourers, depending heavily on agriculture for their livelihood, even after 70 years of Independence without any access to land. In states like Bihar and Andhra Pradesh, SC agricultural labour constitutes as much as 69.36% and 64.36% of total SC workforce respectively in 2011. Similarly, about 78% of the workforce in Bihar and 72.31% of the workforce in Andhra Pradesh depends on agriculture. The incidence of poverty is found to be higher among Dalits than among other groups. There has been an increasing per capita consumer expenditure of all social groups in rural areas at the all-India level during 1987–1988 to 2009–2010. However, there is a significant gap between the per capita consumer expenditure of SC/STs and that of other groups. One important reason for the high incidence of poverty among Dalits, particularly Scheduled Castes, is the high incidence of landlessness and their heavy dependence on agriculture as agricultural labourers. This is due to the failure of the land reforms in Indian agriculture to reduce the levels of inequalities in the distribution of land.

Hence, special measures like the strict implementation of land reforms, the redistribution of surplus land and waste lands among Dalits agricultural labourers and marginal farmers, which must be seen as a priority while the programmes are being implemented. This will improve their economic asset base and skills, particularly education, as it enables them to shift to non-farming employment. The state should also provide the necessary micro finance to augment the productivities of their economic assets.

References

Hanumantha Rao, C.H. (2005). *Agriculture, Food, Security, Poverty and Environment : Essays on Post-Reform India*. Oxford University Press, New Delhi; New York.

Nageswara Rao, B. (1988). Green revolution and land transfers: A case study village in Coastal Andhra. MPhil. dissertation submitted to, Department of Economics University of Hyderabad.

Nancharaiah, G. (1988). *Land and Caste*. Himalaya Publishing House, Bombay.

Nancharaiah, G. (1990, April–June). The Changing position of scheduled castes on agricultural labourers in the labour market. *Social Action*, 40(2), pp. 172–183.

NSSO. (1997). *Household Consumer Expenditure and Employment Situation in India, 53rd Round*. Department of Statistics, Government of India, New Delhi.

NSSO. (2006).*Household Ownership Holdings in India 59th Round (January to December 2003)*. Ministry of Statistics and Programme Implementation, Government of India, New Delhi, p. A-15.

NSSO. (2015). *Household Ownership and Operational Holdings in India*. Ministry of Statistics and Programme Implementation (MOSPI), Government of India, New Delhi, pp. A204–A208.

Rajasekhar, P. (1988). *Land Transfers and Family Partitioning:Historical Case Study of an Andhra Village*. Oxford & IBH Partitioning Co. Pvt. Ltd., New Delhi.

Registrar General and Census Commissioner. (1993). Indian union primary census abstract for scheduled castes and scheduled tribes, paper -1.

Sagar, K. (1988). Land transfer in Uttar Pradesh. *Economic & Political Weekly*, (July 23).

Venkati, B. (1994). Land transfers and alienation in tribal economy: A case study of two selected scheduled area villages of Adilabad districts. Ph.D. Thesis submitted to University of Hyderabad.

4 Land reform and agrarian change

The post-independence period

4.1 Introduction

This chapter examines land reform and agrarian change in the post-Independence period. It is based on secondary data obtained from the NSSO Reports, Agricultural Census 2010–2011. It covers variables such as the distribution of landholdings, changes in the tenancy, terms of lease with special reference to SC/STs and changes in agricultural wages.

The abolition of the intermediary land tenure system was given top priority immediately after Independence as this system was known for its exploitation of tenants. In this system by fixing abnormal rents arbitrarily Jamindars used to extract a surplus from the peasants. As they were required to pay only a fixed amount in the form of land tax to the government; the rest they used to fund their ostentatious lifestyle. They never showed any interest in the development of the land. Tenants also had no incentive to develop the land because they have no control over the piece of land cultivated by them for any stipulated period as it can be taken away by Jamindars at any point of time and leased out to other persons without giving any reasons. Secondly, even if a tenant produced more it was quite likely that it might be appropriated by Jamindar through the collection of high rents in the absence of any rent regulation. On the eve of Independence, about 173 million acres out of 324 million acres of cultivable land were under intermediary tenures. Therefore, it was felt that to protect the interests of the tillers of land, to raise the productivity with equity in the agriculture, and the abolition of intermediary land tenure system as a necessary condition. Accordingly, the Intermediary Land Tenure Abolition Act was promulgated. Jamindars resisted initially by moving the Courts, the government could overcome their resistance through a necessary Constitutional Amendment in early 1951. This tenure was totally abolished, acquiring Jamindars' rights by paying compensation not only to the ownership of land, but also of forests, fisheries and minerals (Dantwala, 1986, pp. 73–74). It should also be noted in this connection that even during the time of the national movement for Independence, the need to abolish the intermediary land tenure system was felt strongly. Although Zamindars were economically powerful, they were politically weak (Nancharaiah, 2001). Furthermore, they were

DOI: 10.4324/9781003147053-4

away from people and land as they were mostly living in urban areas and enjoying their wealth. These factors helped government to overcome the resistance posed by Jamindar in abolishing intermediary tenure. On the eve of Independence more than 40% of the cultivated land was under the control of Jamindars and cultivated by tenants.

This degree of tenancy indicates the degree of feudalism in Indian agriculture on the eve of Independence. It should also be noted that the total food production was 48 million tonnes and population was about 363 million in 1950–1951 (Govt. of India, 1996–1997, pp. S24–S25). About 20 million farmers were conferred on ownership rights at the national level after Jamindari abolition; to this extent, it is definitely a desirable change as land passed from the rentier class, which was an absentee landlord class, to a class of owner cultivators. However, the abolition of Jamindari has some negative aspects from the point of national development. Firstly, a lot of money (Rs. 534 crores) had to be paid in the form of compensation to the erstwhile Jamindars at an average rate of about Rs. 30/- per acre. It varied from Rs. 15/- per acre in Madras composite State to about Rs. 45/- in Bihar. Secondly, a large chunk of land could be retained by Jamindars by claiming as land under personal cultivation and thirdly ownership rights were conferred not to the actual cultivator but to the statutory tenants, that is, persons whose names were recorded as tenants although these tenants have chain of sub-tenants who were actual tillers and belonged to vulnerable sections of society (Dantwala, 1986, p. 74). As a result, many actual tilers who were small and marginal tenants and who belonged to the lower sections of society could not benefit from the abolition of intermediate land tenure. It could help the tenants, who themselves were intermediaries with already some socio-economic base. However, the abolition of intermediary tenure was desirable and successful in terms of removing tenures which were highly inequitable and oppressive and there was an improvement in agrarian relations to this extent.

In the 1950s and 1960s land ceiling acts limiting the size of the farm holding were also promulgated by various states to reduce the inequalities in Indian agriculture. Indian agriculture had also been exposed to new technology from the mid-1960s. New technology refers to the use of high-yielding varieties of seeds, the application of pesticides, chemical fertilizers and the mechanization of agricultural operations. States like Punjab, Haryana, some parts of Andhra Pradesh, Tamil Nadu and Uttar Pradesh, where there was an assured source of irrigation, adapted new technology as it requires continuous irrigation facilities. About 29.1% of the operated area in the country was irrigated in 1981–1982; this proportion increased to 36% in 1991–1992, and then to 44.9% in 2009–2010 (Govt. of India, Ministry of Agriculture, 2009–2010), that is about 45% of operational areas was affected by the green revolution in 2009–2010. In the post-Green Revolution period, there was a tremendous increase in agricultural output, particularly in the area of food production. National food production, which stood at 83 million tonnes in 1960–1961, rose to 108.4 million tonnes in

1970–1971 and then again to 129.4 million tonnes in 1980–1981. This increased further, to 176.4 million tonnes in 1990–1991 and then to 252.02 million tonnes in 2014–2015 (Govt. of India, 2015–2016, p. 100). This increase was mostly due to the intensive cultivation of the area exposed to new technology. But the benefits of the Green Revolution have been cornered by rich farmers as the incomes of those with large holdings increased more than proportionately with the increase in the farm size due to their greater access to modern farm inputs. On the other hand, marginal and small farmers, who did not have similar access to modern farm inputs, were forced to settle for lower incomes. Under farming also traditionally large landowners have appropriated higher incomes in the form of rents while the large mass of sharecroppers and agricultural labourers have received incomes which kept them at a level of subsistence. Thus, the size of the income in rural areas was, by and large, closely related to the amount of land either owned or controlled. It was also evident that in the agriculturally advanced regions there was a substantial increase in the level of money wages and a decline in poverty. It was also found that the incidence of poverty was very low in states like Punjab and Haryana, where the Green Revolution was pervasive, while the incidence of poverty was at a very high level in agriculturally backward states like Bihar and Orissa. Thus, there was an inverse relationship between agricultural growth and the incidence of poverty. However, the income gap between rich and poor has widened in agriculturally advanced regions (Parthasarathy, 1991). And the existing inequalities in the distribution of land was also found to be an important factor for the high incidence of poverty in rural India despite high agricultural growth in the post-Independence period, and particularly in the post-Green Revolution period.

4.2 Land distribution pattern

Let us examine changes in the land distribution pattern of operational holdings in the context of agrarian reform in the post-Independence period. Table 4.1 presents the changing distribution pattern during 1960–1961 to 2012–2013 with respect to operational holdings and operated area at an all-India level.

It could be seen from Table 4.1 that the marginal holdings constitute 38.1% of total holdings, but control only 6.9% of the total operated area in 1960–1961. Small holdings constitute 22.6% of total holdings, but control only 12.3% of total operated area. Marginal and small holdings together constitute nearly 62% of total holdings but control only about 19% of the total operated area in 1960–1961. On the other hand, medium and large holdings together constitute about less than 20% of total holdings, but control more than 60% of the total operated area during the same period.

This indicates that the distribution of land was skewed in 1960–1961. By 2002–2003, there had been a tremendous increase in the number of marginal holdings. Their percentage share in total holdings increased to about 70%,

Table 4.1 Changes in the size distribution of operational holdings and area operated at all India

Category of Holdings	*Percentage distribution of operational holdings and operated area*											
	1960–1961 (17th)		*1970–1971 (26th)*		*1981–1982 (37th)*		*1991–1992 (48th)*		*2002–2003 (59th)*		*2012–2013 (70th)*	
	Nos.	*Area*	*Nos.*	*Area*	*Nos.*	*Area*	*Nos.*	*Area*	*Nos.*	*Area*	*Nos.*	*Area*
Marginal (less than 1.00 ha)	39.1	6.9	45.8	9.2	56.0	11.5	62.8	15.6	69.7	22.6	73.17	27.71
Small (1.01–2.00 ha)	22.6	12.3	22.4	14.8	19.3	16.6	17.8	18.7	16.3	20.9	15.30	23.44
Semi-medium (2.01–10.00 ha)	19.8	20.7	17.7	22.6	14.2	23.6	12.0	24.1	9.0	22.5	8.10	23.50
Medium (4.01–10.00 ha)	14.0	31.2	11.1	30.5	8.6	30.1	6.1	26.4	4.2	22.5	3.04	19.33
Large (larger than 10.00 ha)	4.5	29.0	3.1	23.0	1.9	18.2	1.3	15.2	0.8	11.8	0.37	6.02
All sizes	100	100	100	100	100	100	100	100	100	100	100	100

Sources: NSS Report No. 407 (48th round) 1995, p. 20; NSS report No. 492 (2002–03); NSSO Report No. 571(2013); NSSO Report No. 571(70th round, January–December 2013, p. 36).

but the area operated under their control increased to only less than 23% of total operated area. On the other hand, the number of medium and large holdings declined to about 5% of total holdings, although they accounted for more than 34% of the total area. By 2013, the share of marginal holdings are seen to be marginally increased to 69.7% and control only 27.71% of the total operated area in 2012–2013. On the other hand, the share of medium holdings registered as 3.04% of the total number of holdings, but the area under their control was 19.33% of the operated area. Large holdings have been steadily declined to 0.36% of total holdings, but control 6.02% in 2012–2013. This clearly indicates that although the number of medium and large holdings declined, the area under their control has not declined proportionately. On the other hand, the number of marginal holdings increased from 39% to 77%, but the operated area under their control was less than 28% of the total operated area in 2012–2013. This implies that in the post-Independence period inequalities in the distribution of land has increased despite land reform. The increase in the marginal holdings may be attributed to a population explosion and also to the redistribution of small pieces of surplus land/waste land to weaker sections. But medium and large farmers could retain a large part of operated area as land reforms were not implemented properly. Although the intermediate land tenure system could be effectively removed through Zamindari abolition, equity in the agrarian structure could not be brought. This is for the reason that land has passed hands, that is, from the old absentee landlord (rentier) class to the dominant peasant class, which is the owner cultivator class but land concentration persists. Many micro studies indicated this change in rural India at village level (Nancharaiah, 1988; Shankar, 1988; Rajasekhar, 1988).

The Gini coefficients for operational and ownership holdings (Rural) at the all-India level by NSSO for different years are presented in Table 4.2.

The Gini coefficient increased from 0.583 in 1960–1961 to 0.629 in 1980–1981 and further increased to 0.624 in 2002–2003, before decreasing to 0.516 in 2012–2013 in the case of operational holdings. In the case of

Table 4.2 Gini coefficients for operational and ownership holdings (Rural) at all India

Year	*Operational Holdings*	*Ownership Holdings*
1960–1961	0.583	0.731
1970–1971	0.586	0.709
1980–1981	0.629	0.712
1990–1991	0.641	0.710
2002–2003	0.624	0.741*
2013–2014	0.516	0.72

Sources: NSS Report No. 407 (48th Round, January–December 1992, 1995, p. 22); No. 4922.

*G.S. Bhalla, *Indian agriculture since Independence*, Book Trust India, 2008, New Delhi, p. 37; NSSO Report No. 571 (70th round, January–December. 2013, p. 40).

ownership holdings, the Gini concentration ratio also remained high, that is, 0.72 even in 2013–2014. This indicates a high degree of inequality in the distribution of operational holdings and ownership holdings.

4.3 Growth of landless households

While inequality in the distribution of land was persisting in the case of owned land and operational holdings, at the all-India level, the landlessness has been growing for three decades (1972–2003) and decreasing during the past decade.

From Table 4.3 it follows that the proportion of landless rural households increased from 9.6% to 11.3% during the period 1971 to 1992 at the all-India level. The proportion of landless households remained broadly the same during the later decade, but declined from 10% in 2003 to 7.41% in 2013. Most of the states which showed a high concentration ratio in

Table 4.3 Changes in proportion of landless and Concentration ratio operational holdings (Gini coefficient) (Rural)

	Percentage of landless households					*Concentration ratio in operational holdings*				
STATE	*1972*	*1982*	*1992*	*2003*	*2013*	*71–72*	*1982*	*1992*	*2003*	*2013*
Andhra Pradesh	7.0	11.9	11.9	14.3	22.6	0.582	0.573	0.529	0.543	0.455
Assam	25.0	7.5	13.4	8.1	7.42	0.388	0.465	0.412	0.366	0.351
Bihar	4.3	4.1	8.6	7.6	6.68	0.511	0.534	0.525	0.421	0.376
Chhattisgarh						-	-	-	-	0.361
Gujarat	13.4	16.8	16.3	13.6	12.50	0.518	0.544	0.573	0.605	0.518
Haryana	11.9	6.1	3.7	9.2	1.05	0.436	0.571	0.645	0.675	0.598
Himachal Pradesh	4.4	7.7	10.4	15.0	14.23	-	-	-	-	0.334
Jammu &Kashmir	1.0	6.8	2.8	3.3	3.06	-	-	-	-	0.237
Jharkhand						-	-	-	-	0.35
Karnataka	12.5	13.7	10.0	14.1	10.22	0.509	0.562	0.577	0.543	0.509
Kerala	15.7	12.8	8.4	4.8	9.35	0.483	0.449	0.392	0.348	0.342
Madhya Pradesh	9.6	14.4	15.2	12.1	13.79	0.508	0.52	0.533	0.527	0.508
Maharashtra	10.4	21.2	19.6	17.7	12.84	0.514	0.57	0.57	0.526	0.474
Orissa	10.6	7.7	13.8	9.6	5.39	0.466	0.504	0.462	0.381	0.316
Punjab	7.1	6.4	5.9	4.6	6.84	0.398	0.685	0.694	0.706	0.67
Rajasthan	2.9	8.1	6.4	5.7	3.89	0.599	0.551	0.59	0.61	0.575
Tamil Nadu	17.0	19.1	17.9	16.6	8.84	0.48	0.555	0.527	0.508	0.48
Telangana						-	-	-	-	0.44
Uttar Pradesh	4.6	4.9	4.9	3.8	3.32	0.471	0.52	0.498	0.45	0.444
West Bengal	9.8	16.2	11.0	6.2	6.55	0.433	0.494	0.43	0.313	0.223
All India	9.6	11.3	11.3	10.0	7.41	0.567	0.596	0.591	0.557	0.516

Source: NSSO Report No. 571 (70th round, January–December 2013, p. 27).

operational holdings have also reported a high proportion of landless households between 1972 to 2003. In the case of Andhra Pradesh, landless households increased from 7% in 1972 to 14.3% in 2003 and the concentration ratio declined marginally, from 0.582 to 0.543 during the same period. However, the landlessness ratio substantially increased from 14.3% in 2003 to 22.6% in 2013 and the concentration ratio declined marginally from 0.543 in 2003 to 0.455 in 2013, while the national concentration ratio also declined marginally from 0.557 to 0.516 during the same period. At the all-India level, the percentage of landless households (7.41%) in 2013 was the lowest recorded in the past five decades. The percentage of landless households had initially increased from 9.6% in 1972 to 11.3 in 1982, remained the same in 1992 and thereafter declined to 10% in 2003, and further declined to 7.4% in 2013. Within the major states, no distinct pattern of increasing or declining was observed in the percentage of landless households until 1992. However, after 1992 all the major states revealed a declining percentage of landless households, with the exception of Andhra Pradesh, Himachal Pradesh, Kerala and Punjab, where the proportion of landless households has increased.

4.4 Changes in the tenancy

Now let us examine the changes in the tenancy in term of changes in the proportion of leased-in households and the percentage of area leased in total area owned as indicators of incidence of tenancy.

It is evident from Table 4.4 that there is a declining trend in the percentage of leased-in households and the percentage of leased-in area out of the total owned area during 1971–1972 to 2003 and again increasing during the period 2003–2013. The percentage of leased-in households raised from 12% in 2003 to 14% in 2013.The ratio of area leased-in declined from 12% in 1971–1972 to 7% in 2003 but raised to 12% in 2013. It is also observed from the table that there was a declining trend in the percentage of area leased-out to the total area owned over the three decades, although an increase was observed in 2013. However, the gap between area leased-in and area leased-out is very high. The reason may be that there is a tendency to suppress information on the leasing-out of land among the landowners,

Table 4.4 Estimates of reported incidence of leasing out and leasing in of land by households from various rounds of NSSO

Item	*1971–1972*	*1982*	*1992*	*2003*	*2013*
Percentage of households leasing in land	25	18	15	12	14
Percentage of area leased-in to total area owned	12	7	9	7	12
Percentage of area leased-out to total area owned	6	4	5	3	4

Sources: NSSO Report No. 571 (70th round, January–December 2013, p. 29).

Table 4.5 Incidence of tenancy for 20 major states in 2012–2013

States	*Percentage of households reporting*		*Average area leased in per reporting household (ha)*	*Leased-in area as percent of total area owned*
	Leased-out land	*Leased-in land*		
Andhra Pradesh	4.64	37.21	0.779	59.03
Assam	1.78	7.04	0.397	4.5
Bihar	3.11	18.72	0.395	30.71
Chhattisgarh	3.46	13.66	0.537	9.3
Gujarat	2.1	6.15	0.833	6.38
Haryana	5.48	12.94	0.963	16.38
Himachal Pradesh	4.91	21.17	0.102	5.47
Jammu & Kashmir	0.52	3.03	0.034	0.24
Jharkhand	2.64	5.9	0.178	2.18
Karnataka	6.02	8.64	0.687	6.99
Kerala	2.01	14.29	0.148	10.26
Madhya Pradesh	2.14	5.61	1.081	5.41
Maharashtra	0.9	8.41	0.383	3.6
Odisha	4.82	19.28	0.403	20.47
Punjab	5.25	15.77	1.157	29.1
Rajasthan	5.22	7.56	1.242	6.36
Tamil Nadu	1.91	13.16	0.4	15.03
Telangana	1.2	16.45	0.793	18.59
Uttar Pradesh	3.9	10.64	0.394	8.61
West Bengal	3.57	17.8	0.167	17.29
N E States	2.62	12.65	0.227	4.08
Group of UTs	1	27.53	0.282	54.52
All India	3.26	13.65	0.501	11.62

Sources: NSSO Report No. 571 (70th round, January–December, 2013 p. 30).

owing to the fear of tenancy legislation. Hence, the proportion of leasing-in households and the proportion of area leased-in are used as indicators of the incidences of tenancy.

From Table 4.5 it is observed that at the all-India level, 3.26% of households reported leased-out land and 13.65% of households reported leased-in land in 2012–2013. The average leased-in area per reporting household was 0.5 hectares, while the leased-in area as a percentage of the total area owned was 11.62% in 2012–2013. Among the major states the highest percentage of leased-in households was reported in Andhra Pradesh (37.21%), and the lowest was reported in Jammu & Kashmir (3.03%). The proportion of leased-in area was highest in Andhra Pradesh (59.03%), while the lowest proposition was reported in Jammu & Kashmir. The national average percentage of the leased-in area was 11.62. In the case of households leasing-out, Karnataka registered highest (6.02%), followed by Haryana (5.48%) while the lowest was registered in Jammu & Kashmir (0.52%).

When we examine the changes in the incidence of tenancy in terms of operational holdings and operated area we find the same declining trends in terms of leased-in area and leased-in households for four decades during 1970–1971 to 2002–2003 and increasing during 2003–2013. The holdings operating on leased-in area (tenant holding) declined sharply from 25.7% to 9.9% during the same period, but raised to 13.7% in 2012–2013. The extent of leased-in area declined from 10.6% in 1970–1971 to 6.5% in 2002–2003 in rural India. However, over the last decade, it has risen to 11% in 2013.

It is observed from the Table 4.6 that the percentages of tenant holdings of all categories declined over the past four decades (1970–1971 to 2002–2003). However, it should be noted that all categories of holdings registered an increase over the last decade and the increase is very significant in the case of semi-medium, medium and large holdings. There was a steady decline in the proportion of tenanted area under all sizes during 1960–1961 to 2002–2003, but it increased to 11% in 2013.

4.5 Incidence of tenancy: inter-state variation

It can be seen from Table 4.7 that the percentage of tenant holdings was highest in Andhra Pradesh (42.3%) among the 20 major states in 2012–2013, while it was at its lowest in Jammu & Kashmir (0.01%). For the country as a whole, the proportion of tenant holdings declined from 15.2% to 9.9% during 1981–1982 to 2002–2003 and it increased to 13.7% in 2012–2013. The share of leased-in area increased from 7.2% in 1981–1982 to 10.2% in 2012–2013 at the all-India level. Most of the states conformed to this pattern, with the exception of a few states such as Maharashtra and Uttar Pradesh during 2012–2013. At the all-India level, the percentage of tenant holdings and leased-in area declined substantially, from 15.2% in 1981–1982 to 9.9% in 2002–2003 and increased to 13.7% in 2012–2013. In 2012–2013, the percentage of holdings has increased for all categories of holdings while the large holdings accounted for the highest percentage of increase, that is 21.8% in 2012–2013 (Table 4.6).

Thus, the analysis of changes in the land distribution in the context of agrarian reform in the post-Independence period, shows clearly that inequalities in the distribution of land measured in terms of the Gini concentration ratio declined marginally from 0.567% in 1970–1971 to 0.516% in 2012–2013 in the case of operational holdings, but remained the same (at 7.12%) in the case of ownership holdings. There has been a substantial decline in the incidence of tenancy in terms of the percentage of tenant holdings and the percentages of tenanted area during 1971–1972 to 2002–2003, but increased in 2012–2013. The leased-in area also increased under all categories of holdings in the last decade. The increase is very significant in the case of large holdings in terms of tenanted holdings

Table 4.6 Percentage of tenant holdings and area leased-in by category of operational holdings at all India level

Category of operational holdings	*Percentage of tenant holdings*					*Percentage of area leased-in*				2012–2013	
	1970–1971	1981–1982	1991–1992	2002–2003	2012–2013	1970–1971	1981–1982	1991–1992	2002–2003	*July 2012–December 2012*	*January 2013–June 2013*
Marginal	27	14.4	9.3	9.8	13.2	18.9	9.7	8.7	8.6	10.73	11.3
Small	27.8	17.9	14.9	10.7	13.6	14.6	8.5	8.5	6.8	9.85	11.25
Semi-Medium	24.8	15.9	12.2	10.3	18	11.7	7.3	7.4	6.3	10.01	13.14
Medium	20	14.5	13.1	7.8	14.8	8.7	6.6	6.9	4.2	9.52	8.64
Large	15.9	11.5	16.7	13.8	21.8	5.9	5.3	11.4	6.1	12.25	12.59
All	25.7	15.2	11	9.9	13.7	10.6	7.2	8.3	6.5	10.22	11.3

Sources: NSSO Report No. 571 (70th round, January–December 2013, p. 43).

Table 4.7 Percentage of tenant holdings and operated area leased-in for 20 major states

	Percentage of Tenant Holdings				*Percentage Share of Leased-in Area*			
States	*1981–1982*	*1991–1992*	*2001–2002*	*2012–2013*	*1981–1982*	*1991–1992*	*2001–2002*	*2012–2013*
Andhra Pradesh	13.8	14.1	12.9	42.3	6.2	9.6	9	34.2
Assam	12.9	10.1	8.9	8	6.4	8.9	5.3	4.3
Bihar	19.7	5.6	12.7	28	10.3	3.9	8.9	21.6
Chhattisgarh	12	9.5						
Gujarat	4.8	3.7	5.3	6.1	2	3.3	5.1	5.6
Haryana	25.9	17.1	10.7	15.1	18.2	33.7	14.4	15
Himachal Pradesh	-	-	-	10.5	-	-	-	5.2
Jammu &Kashmir	-	-	-	0.3	-	-	-	0.1
Jharkhand	-	-	-	4.4	-	-	-	1.9
Karnataka	10.7	8	4.6	5.1	6	7.4	3.6	6.7
Kerala	6.7	5.2	5.1	10.6	2.6	2.9	4	8.3
Madhya Pradesh	8	9	7.3	6.4	3.6	6.3	3.6	5
Maharashtra	10.6	6.9	6.6	4.4	5.2	5.5	4.7	3.4
Odisha	18.2	16.9	19.4	20.6	9.9	9.5	13	16.7
Punjab	21.3	15.9	13.1	19	16.1	18.8	16.8	24.8
Rajasthan	7.1	6.5	2.9	7.6	4.3	5.2	2.8	7.8
Tamil Nadu	24.7	15.3	9.4	13	10.9	10.9	6	14.3
Telangana	-	-	-	18.4	-	-	-	13.7
Uttar Pradesh	20.5	15.5	11.7	10.6	10.2	10.5	9.5	7.6
West Bengal	23.1	14.4	14.1	21.7	12.3	10.4	9.3	14.6
All India	15.2	11	9.9	13.7	7.2	8.3	6.5	10.2

Source: NSSO Report No. 571 (70th round, January–December 2013, p. 42).

4.6 Terms of lease

The leasing of land is contracted by two parties under certain terms of lease that are binding on both parties. Leased-in land was classified by terms of lease for (i) fixed money, (ii) fixed produce, (iii) share of produce, (iv) under service contract, (v) share of produce together with other terms, (vi) under usufructuary mortgage, (vii) from relatives under no specific terms, and (viii) under other terms. The percentage distribution of leased-in operated area under first three specific terms of lease are presented, and the rest are put together as 'others' (Table 4.11). It is to be noted from Table 4.11 that fixed money (41.1%) was found to be the most prevalent practice of leasing land followed by share of produce (28.7%) and fixed produce (17.0%) (Table 4.8).

It is seen that, over the past five decades, the terms of lease against share of produce is slowly losing importance, whereas fixed money as terms of lease is increasingly gaining importance.

Table 4.8 Trends in the percentage distribution of leased-in operated area by terms of lease across the last five LHS surveys of NSS

Terms of lease	*1970–1971*	*1981–1982*	*1991–1992*	*2002–2003*	*2012–2013*
Fixed money	15.4	10.9	19	29.5	41.1
Fixed produce	11.6	6.3	14.5	20.3	17
Share of Produce	47.9	41.9	34.4	40.3	28.7
Others	25.1	40.9	32.1	9.9	12.9
All terms	100	100	100	100	100

Source: NSSO Report No. 571 (70th round, January–December 2013).

4.7 Inter-state variation in leasing under different terms

It can be seen from Table 4.9 that in Punjab and Haryana, the two most agriculturally advanced states in the country, the most prevalent form of contract was fixed money. In Punjab, about 94.5% of the tenanted land was contracted for fixed money during the period July 2012–December 2012 and 93.7% in January 2013–June 2013. In Haryana, about 79.5% of the tenanted land was contracted for fixed money in July 2012–December 2012 and 75.8% during January 2013–June 2013.

Share of produce was found to be the most predominant form of tenancy in Assam (67.0% in July 2012–December 2012 and 55.8% in January 2013–June 2013) and in Karnataka (63.4% in July 2012–December 2012 and 50.3% in January 2013–Jun 2013). Fixed produce was reported as the most common form of tenancy in terms of leased-in area in Chhattisgarh (57.8% during July 2012–December 2012 and 61.6% during January 2013–June 2013) while share of produce and fixed money tenancies were the main terms of leasing in most of the states. Leasing in from relatives under no specific terms was very common in Himachal Pradesh (52.0% during July 2012–Dec ember 2012 and 46.2% during January 2013–June 2013) and Kerala (36.4% during July 2012–December 2012 and 30.0% during January 2013–Jun 2013).

4.8 Terms of lease among SCs/STs across the states

Table 4.10 presents the distribution of area leased-in according to different terms of leasing for the holdings of Scheduled Castes showed that share of produce was the most dominant term of leasing, as about 62.0% of leased-in area fell under this category at the all-India level. The only states with a higher proportion than the all-India average of 61.86% were Chhattisgarh (100.0%), where the entire leased-in area fell under this category, followed by Tripura (86.5%), West Bengal (86.1%), Madhya Pradesh (76.8%) and Odisha (68.4%). The state of Assam had also as high as 58.3% of leased-in area under share of produce. The other states which had a substantial proportion of leased-in area under this category were Bihar (28.9%), Goa (21.0%), Himachal Pradesh (17.9%), Jammu & Kashmir

Table 4.9 Percentage distribution of leased in operated area by terms of lease for major states

	Percentage of area by terms of lease (July 2012–December 2012)						*Percentage of area by terms of lease (January 2013–June 2013)*					
States	*Fixed money*	*Fixed produce*	*Share of produce*	*Relatives under no specific terms*	*Others*	*All (incl n. r.)*	*Fixed money*	*Fixed produce*	*Share of produce*	*Relatives under no specific terms*	*Others*	*All (incl n. r.)*
Andhra Pradesh	60.9	25	9.1	4.6	0.4	100	51.9	20.9	21.2	4.4	1.4	100
Assam	13.4	9.8	67	6.1	3.4	100	17.3	10.9	55.8	6	2.6	100
Bihar	24.1	36.5	35.1	0.3	4	100	24.6	27.5	35.6	0.4	3	100
Chhattisgarh	3.3	57.8	21.9	7.6	9.3	100	5.3	61.6	21.3	8.2	0.4	100
Gujarat	24.9	0	48.6	25.7	0.8	100	12	0	57.6	29.3	1	100
Haryana	79.5	7.8	2.1	9.7	1	100	75.8	8.7	1.9	10.7	1.2	100
Himachal Pradesh	28.5	2.1	6.5	52	11	100	31.4	1	7	46.2	12.4	100
Jammu & Kashmir	0	0	11.2	19.3	53.6	100	0.4	0	10.2	11.1	30.5	100
Jharkhand	15.4	33.6	31.7	0	0	100	17.4	7	72.2	0	0	100
Karnataka	17	14.7	63.4	2.7	2.1	100	34.4	8.4	50.3	2.7	3.9	100
Kerala	39.8	11.5	6.5	36.4	5.9	100	39.4	9.7	8.7	30	6.2	100
Madhya Pradesh	14.4	9.8	42.5	16.9	16.5	100	16.8	10.4	35.8	15.7	20	100
Maharashtra	54.7	1.8	27.3	7.6	8.5	100	43.6	3.5	29	8.4	4.2	100
Odisha	6.9	24.3	45.2	5.3	13.8	100	9.5	27.6	58.3	1.1	2.9	100
Punjab	94.5	1	1.9	1.2	1.4	100	93.7	1.4	1.9	1.2	1.3	100
Rajasthan	29.5	8.6	46.5	12.2	3.2	100	52.8	5.9	25	9.9	3.7	100
Tamil Nadu	63.2	7.4	6.9	20.7	1.7	100	72.3	6.6	5.7	13.3	2.1	100
Telangana	65.6	6.6	27.2	0.6	0	100	55.8	5.9	35.1	0.3	1.1	100
Uttar Pradesh	26.9	13.2	36.9	5.6	17.3	100	24.2	9.5	35.6	5.2	21.2	100
West Bengal	24.7	15.5	49.1	5.6	5	100	39.3	15.8	34.6	2.2	5.5	100
N E States	25.2	23	25.3	17.9	8.7	100	28.5	10.7	11.7	24.3	9	100
Group of UTs	7.8	6.7	63	22.3	0.2	100	10.5	5.9	70.5	12.7	0.4	100
All India	41.1	17	28.7	7.6	5.3	100	41.9	15.1	28.4	6.2	5.5	100

Source: NSSO Report No. 571 (70th round, January–December 2013).

Table 4.10 State-wise distribution of leased-in area of Scheduled Castes by terms of leasing, 2010–2011 (Area in ha.)

States/UTs	*Fixed money*	*Fixed produce*	*Share of produce*	*Usufructuary mortgage*	*Other terms*	*Total*
Andhra Pradesh	2547	829	62	0	0	3438
	74.1	24.11	1.79	0	0	100
Arunachal	0	0	0	0	0	0
Pradesh	0	0	0	0	0	0
Assam	0	25	70	25	0	119
	0	20.66	58.26	21.08	0	100
Bihar	228	173	171	19	0	591
	38.6	29.23	28.94	3.23	0	100
Chhattisgarh	0	0	48	0	0	48
	0	0	100	0	0	100
Goa	4	6	3	0	0	13
	31.19	47.79	21.02	0	0	100
Himachal	114	51	179	40	618	1002
Pradesh	11.41	5.1	17.85	3.95	61.69	100
Jammu &	14	46	13	0	0	73
Kashmir	18.8	63.83	17.38	0	0	100
Jharkhand	37	45	33	0	0	114
	32.12	39.29	28.59	0	0	100
Kerala	847	151	201	10	124	1334
	63.53	11.36	15.04	0.76	9.31	100
Madhya Pradesh	105	316	1394	0	0	1815
	5.81	17.39	76.8	0	0	100
Manipur	0	490	0	31	0	521
	0	94.06	0	5.94	0	100
Odisha	12439	22605	77998	755	231	114028
	10.91	19.82	68.4	0.66	0.2	100
Punjab	3168	330	5	6	0	3509
	90.28	9.41	0.15	0.17	0	100
Rajasthan	15744	1517	5065	11	1115	23453
	67.13	6.47	21.6	0.05	4.75	100
Sikkim	3	101	0	0	0	104
	2.78	97.22	0	0	0	100
Tamil Nadu	1355	1749	250	289	85	3728
	36.35	46.91	6.7	7.76	2.28	100
Tripura	23	10	208	0	0	241
	9.38	4.17	86.46	0	0	100
Uttarakhand	202	35	4	1	23	266
	76.09	13.22	1.39	0.5	8.8	100
Uttar Pradesh	31414	2978	1	0	8	34401
	91.32	8.66	Neg	0	0.02	100
West Bengal	9399	6073	110418	1403	917	128210
	7.33	4.74	86.12	1.09	0.72	100
All India	77653	37555	196134	2591	3121	317055
	24.49	11.85	61.86	0.82	0.98	100

Source: Agricultural Census, 2010–2011.

(17.4%), Jharkhand (28.6%), Kerala (15.0%), Rajasthan (21.6%) and Puducherry (28.2%). The fixed money was the second important term of leasing, having a share of 24.5% at the all-India level among states. Uttar Pradesh (91.3%) has the highest proportion of leased-in area under this category, followed by Punjab (90.3%), Uttarakhand (76.1%), Andhra Pradesh (74.1%), Rajasthan (67.1%), Kerala (63.5%), Bihar (38.6%), Tamil Nadu (36.4%), Jharkhand (32.1%) and Goa (31.2%). In terms of fixed produce, the proportion of leased-in area above the national average of 11.85% was found in the states of Andhra Pradesh (24.1%), Assam (20.7%), Bihar (29.2%), Goa (47.8%), Jammu & Kashmir (63.8%), Jharkhand (39.3%), Madhya Pradesh (17.4%), Manipur (94.1%), Odisha (19.8%), Sikkim (97.2%), Tamil Nadu (46.9%), Uttarakhand (13.2%) and Puducherry (51.1%). The operated area under usufructuary mortgage and 'other terms' was less than 1.0% each at the all-India level, but was as high as 21.1% in Assam, followed by Tamil Nadu (7.8%) and Manipur (5.9%) (Table 4.11).

Like the holdings of all social groups and Scheduled Castes, 'share of produce' was the most dominant term of leasing of area operated for Scheduled Tribes as well, which is evident from the fact that 57.60% of the leased-in area belonged to this category at the all-India level. In Chhattisgarh and Nagaland, entire leased-in area (100.0%) fell under this category, followed by West Bengal (82.3%), Madhya Pradesh (74.6%), Assam and Tripura (70.8% each), Odisha (49.2%)and Goa (44.9%). The next important term of leasing of area was under 'fixed money', having a share of 21.7% at the all-India level. The highest proportion of leased-in area under this category was reported in Andhra Pradesh (86.6%) followed by Jharkhand (83.2%), Uttar Pradesh (68.3%), Rajasthan (55.4%), Jammu & Kashmir (53.4%), Goa (41.6%), Bihar (37.4%), Odisha (23.5%), Sikkim (23.0%), Kerala (15.3%) and West Bengal (10.1%). The proportion of leased-in area under 'fixed produce' was 16.2% at the all-India level and was the highest in Manipur (100.0%), followed by Meghalaya (76.5%), Bihar (62.6%), Sikkim (57.8%), Jammu & Kashmir (46.3%), Uttar Pradesh (31.7%), Tripura (25.4%), Odisha (24.3%), Madhya Pradesh (18.8%), Assam (16.0%), Goa (13.4%) etc. The proportions of leased-in area under 'usufructuary mortgaged' and 'others' were 2.3%, each at the all-India level.

4.9 Changes in average agricultural wage rate during 2005–2006 to 2015–2016

It follows from Tables 4.12 & 4.13 that the average agricultural wages rate for field labour (male and also female) has been increasing during the period 2005–2006 to 2015–2016 at the all-India level and also across the states. Both male and female field labour were paid the highest wage (Rs.576 and Rs.427 respectively) in Kerala in 2015–2016, while the lowest wage for male field labour was paid (Rs.176) in Gujarat and for female field labour the lowest was paid (Rs.134) in Chhattisgarh during the same year.

Table 4.11 State-wise distribution of leased-in area of Scheduled Tribes by terms of leasing, 2010–2011

States/UTs	*Fixed money*	*Fixed produce*	*Share of produce*	*Usufructuary mortgage*	*Other terms*	*Total*
Andhra	3264	283	212	0	11	3769
Pradesh	86.6	7.51	5.62	0	0.28	100
Assam	0	10	43	8	0	60
	0	16.01	70.82	13.18	0	100
Bihar	19	31	0	0	0	50
	37.38	62.62	0	0	0	100
Chhattisgarh	0	0	1260	0	0	1260
	0	0	100	0	0	100
Goa	1329	428	1434	0	0	3191
	41.64	13.42	44.93	0	0	100
Himachal	0	1	3	7	27	37
Pradesh	0	1.81	7.75	17.61	72.83	100
Jammu &	60	52	0	0	0	113
Kashmir	53.42	46.33	0.25	0	0	100
Jharkhand	199	2	38	0	0	240
	83.2	0.81	15.99	0	0	100
Kerala	270	10	76	0	1413	1768
	15.27	0.56	4.29	0	79.88	100
Madhya	130	386	1531	6	0	2052
Pradesh	6.33	18.8	74.6	0.28	0	100
Manipur	0	41	0	0	0	41
	0	100	0	0	0	100
Meghalaya	15	145	30	0	0	189
	7.83	76.51	15.66	0	0	100
Nagaland	0	0	1876	0	0	1876
	0	0	100	0	0	100
Odisha	17727	18344	37120	1180	1143	75514
	23.48	24.29	49.16	1.56	1.51	100
Punjab	0	0	0	0	0	0
	0	0	0	0	0	0
Rajasthan	2279	316	337	1001	179	4112
	55.42	7.69	8.2	24.35	4.35	100
Sikkim	81	203	54	0	14	352
	22.98	57.8	15.37	0	3.86	100
Tamil Nadu	0	0	0	0	0	0
	0	0	0	0	0	0
Tripura	64	423	1178	0	0	1664
	3.82	25.39	70.79	0	0	100
Uttarakhand	0	0	0	0	5	5
	0	0	0	0	100	100
Uttar Pradesh	798	371	0	0	0	1168
	68.27	31.73	0	0	0	100
West Bengal	4479	1853	36469	1074	439	44314
	10.11	4.18	82.29	2.42	0.99	100
All India	30713	22898	81659	3276	3229	141776
	21.66	16.15	57.6	2.31	2.28	100

Source: Agricultural Census, 2010–2011.

Table 4.12 State-wise average agricultural wage rate for field labour (male) – 2005–2006 to 2015–2016

States	*2005–2006*	*2006–2007*	*2007–2008*	*2008–2009*	*2009–2010*	*2010–2011*	*2011–2012*	*2012–2013*	*2013–2014*	*2014–2015*	*2015–2016*
Andhra	62	69	85	108	128	162	194	227	245	277	295
Assam	66	69	79	81	96	118	142	177	209	242	245
Bihar	60	71	71	84	87	129	140	185	191	205	215
Chhattisgarh	48	52	58	71	75	85	117	125	150	176	181
Gujarat	76	77	82	94	102	118	137	148	161	195	176
Haryana	111	115	129	164	195	224	266	301	339	372	388
Himachal	85	99	102	119	129	158	177	196	209	247	276
Jharkhand	NA	61	81	83	92	106	104	119	155	NA	182
Karnataka	68	72	78	114	115	130	171	181	224	279	272
Kerala	163	183	201	227	264	306	364	433	486	535	576
Madhya	55	56	59	74	87	103	131	155	175	187	213
Maharashtra	54	50	67	71	82	100	121	175	120	152	NA
Orissa	48	56	56	65	81	102	124	149	171	197	224
Punjab	99	98	107	132	159	201	276	281	304	338	373
Rajasthan	72	91	102	116	139	148	184	207	231	275	300
Tamil	76	76	93	103	129	160	196	245	253	303	334
Tripura	NA	105	NA	NA	NA	188	222	255	273	285	288
Uttar	70	67	88	91	104	124	151	180	203	226	238
West	62	67	74	82	98	130	157	267	214	231	259
All India Average	74	82	91	108	124	149	183	214	229	268	281

Source: *Agricultural Wages in India 2015–2016*, Directorate of Economics And Statistics, Department of Agriculture, Cooperation & Farmers Welfare, Ministry of Agriculture & Farmers Welfare, Government of India, New Delhi, pp. 4–5.

Table 4.13 State-wise average agricultural wage rate for field labour (female) – 2005–2006 to 2015–2016

States	*2005–2006*	*2006–2007*	*2007–2008*	*2008–2009*	*2009–2010*	*2010–2011*	*2011–2012*	*2012–2013*	*2013–2014*	*2014–2015*	*2015–2016*
Andhra Pradesh	44	50	62	79	95	124	141	159	179	195	200
Assam	48	45	52	60	-	95	114	138	166	190	200
Bihar	47	58	68	68	68	112	115	166	171	194	203
Chhattisgarh	36	36	44	52	60	66	88	88	104	124	134
Gujarat	62	65	71	83	92	107	123	132	144	161	156
Haryana	90	93	101	138	165	184	215	255	290	308	322
Himachal	83	80	86	102	106	128	148	171	188	228	252
Jharkhand	NA	58	63	79	87	100	99	111	141	NA	170
Karnataka	60	68	74	110	111	125	152	161	202	235	245
Kerala	108	117	138	165	193	236	283	336	375	405	427
Madhya	46	48	52	64	76	92	118	137	152	162	184
Maharashtra	40	46	67	59	65	80	93	125	94	100	NA
Orissa	47	43	46	55	64	80	94	116	127	150	173
Rajasthan	53	64	75	84	82	90	118	155	182	217	247
Tamil	39	42	45	56	68	83	97	112	123	130	142
Tripura	87	84	NA	NA	NA	140	159	183	202	217	225
Uttar Pradesh	NA	60	78	76	98	NA	131	154	180	191	216
West	52	54	69	67	83	110	132	146	181	186	219
All-India Average	59	62	70	82	95	115	134	158	178	200	218

Source: *Agricultural Wages in India 2015–2016*, Directorate of Economics and Statistics, Department of Agriculture, Cooperation & Farmers Welfare, Ministry of Agriculture & Farmers Welfare, Government of India, New Delhi, p. 5.

At the all-India level, the annual average wage rate for male and female for field labour was Rs. 281 and Rs. 218, respectively, in 2015–2016. That is, male workers were paid 29 per cent more than female workers. Among the states, the gender gap, in term of wages, is also observed. In Tamil Nadu, the gender gap is highest (136%) while it is lowest in Bihar (6%).

4.10 Conclusion

Various land reform measures have been initiated to reduce the inequalities in the distribution of land, to provide security to tenants and to raise the productivity of agriculture in the post-Independence period. Land reform was successful to the extent of removing of intermediaries like Jamindars, Jagirdars and Inamdars and significantly reducing the incidence of tenancy. However, land concentration persists in the post-reform period. Because land passed hands, that is, from rentier class to owner cultivator class but land reform did not benefit the marginal farmers and agricultural labourers who mostly come from socially disadvantaged sections such as Dalits. From the mid-1960s onwards, Indian agriculture has been exposed to new technology, the development popularly known as the Green Revolution. As a result, the agricultural growth rate increased substantially, particularly in the area of food production. But the incidence of poverty continues to be high at the national level, despite the high growth rate in the area of food production. One important reason for this is that the gains of the Green Revolution have been mostly cornered by the better-off farmers. But marginal farmers and agricultural labourers could not make significant gains due to their low or no land base. Of course, the incidence of poverty is found to be low in agriculturally advanced states such as Punjab and Haryana compared to backward states like Orissa, Bihar and Madhya Pradesh.

It is also found that the gap between marginal farmers, agricultural labourers and rich farmers in terms of monthly per capita consumption is wider in agriculturally advanced states than in agriculturally backward states.

In the post-Independence period although the incidence of tenancy has declined during 1971–1972 to 2002–2003, it increased in 2012–2013. The inverse relationship between the size of holding and the incidence of tenancy is found to have disappeared at a national level as a tenanted area under marginal holdings declined and large holdings which constituted one-fifth of the total holdings control two-thirds of the total tenanted area in the 1980s.

Regarding terms of leases, the dominant form of lease was 'fixed money' followed by 'share of produce' and 'fixed produce' while in the case of SC/STs 'share of produce' has the dominant form of terms of lease, followed by 'fixed money' and 'fixed produce'.

References

Dantwala, M. L. (1986). *Indian Agricultural Development Since Independence: A Collection of Essays*. Oxford and IBH Publishing Co, New Delhi, p. 519. ISBN 8120401182.

Government of India, Ministry of Finance, New Delhi, Economic Survey 2007–2008.

Government of India, Statistics of Indian Agriculture, Ministry of Agriculture 2015–2016, p. 100.

Nancharaiah, G.(1988). *Land and Caste*. Himalaya Publishing House, Bombay.

Nancharaiah, G. (2001). Artha Vijnana. *Journal of The Gokhale Institute of Politics and Economics*, 43(1–2), p. 193, June. DOI:10.21648/arthavij/2001/v43/i1-2/115857

Prathasarathy, G. (1991). HYV technology: The polarisation and immiserisation controversy. *Economic Political Weekly*, 26(26), June 29, ISSN (Print) - 0012-9976

Shankar, K. (1988). Land transfer in Uttar Pradesh. *Economic & Political Weekly*, (July 23).

5 Employment and unemployment situation among different social groups at the all-India and state level

5.1 Introduction

This chapter attempts to examine the employment and unemployment situation among different social groups at the all-India level and across the states. It is based on secondary data obtained from the employment–unemployment scenario among different social groups 2013–2014, according to the Government of India's Ministry of Labour & Employment Labour Bureau. It covers the unemployment rate, the underemployment rate and the labour force participation rate among different social groups with special reference to gender.

5.2 Unemployment rate for persons aged 15 years and above according to the Usual Principal Status (UPS) approach (in %)

Based on the UPS[1] approach, the unemployment rate at the all-India level (rural + urban) is 5.3% under the others category, which is the highest among all of the four social groups. In the case of OBC, the unemployment rate is estimated to be 4.8%, followed by 4.6% under SC category and the lowest (4.5%) under the ST category in 2013–2014 (Table 5.1).

In the case of rural areas, the ST category has the lowest unemployment rate, i.e., 4.3%, whereas it is highest in the others category (5.3%). In urban areas, the unemployment rate is lowest under the OBC (5.3%) category, while it is the highest in the case of SC Category (5.8%)

While comparing gender-wise unemployment rate (Rural + Urban) at the all-India level under the UPS approach there is a wide variation between the male and female unemployment rates. In the case of females, the maximum unemployment rate is estimated to be 10.5% (under the others category) whereas for males the same is 4.2%, under the same social group. In urban areas, the unemployment rate among females is highest (14.5%) in the case of others, while it is lowest in the case of STs females (9.5%) and in the case of SC females it is 10.7%.

Table 5.2 shows that at the national level (rural + urban) based on Usual Principal and Subsidiary Status[2] (UPSS) unemployment rate in case of ST category is 2.1% followed by 3.1% under SC.

DOI: 10.4324/9781003147053-5

Table 5.1 Unemployment rate for persons aged 15 years & above according to Usual Principal Status Approach (ps) (in%)

	Rural			*Urban*			*Rural + Urban*		
Particulars	*M*	*F*	*P*	*M*	*F*	*P*	*M*	*F*	*P*
SC	3.9	5.7	4.4	4.5	10.7	5.8	4.0	6.6	4.6
ST	4.0	5.1	4.3	4.4	9.5	5.5	4.0	5.5	4.5
OBC	4.1	6.4	4.7	3.8	11.5	5.3	4.0	7.6	4.8
Others	4.5	8.3	5.2	3.8	14.5	5.6	4.2	10.5	5.3

Source: Government of India, *Employment–Unemployment Scenario among Different Social Groups*, Vol. I, 2013–2014, p. 15.

Table 5.2 Unemployment rate for persons aged 15 years & above according to Usual Principal & Subsidiary Status Approach (PS + SS) (in %)

	Rural			*Urban*			*Rural + Urban*		
Particulars	*M*	*F*	*P*	*M*	*F*	*P*	*M*	*F*	*P*
SC	2.7	2.7	2.7	3.9	8.9	5.0	2.9	3.6	3.1
ST	1.9	1.7	1.8	3.6	7.6	4.6	2.2	2.1	2.1
OBC	2.7	3.6	2.9	3.4	10.0	4.8	2.9	4.9	3.4
Others	3.2	5.4	3.7	3.5	13.1	5.1	3.3	7.8	4.2

Source: Government of India, *Employment–Unemployment Scenario among Different Social Groups*, Vol. I, 2013–2014, p. 16.

Category, 3.4% under the OBC category while under the others category there is highest unemployment rate (4.2%). The highest unemployment rate in both rural and urban areas is to be found in the others category, whereas the ST category shows the lowest unemployment rate in both areas.

The female unemployment rate (rural + urban) is higher than the male unemployment in the case of all four social groups, except ST. Under the ST category, the female unemployment rate is 2.1%, whereas in the male category it is 2.2%. In the case of others, the female unemployment rate is more than double (7.8%) the unemployment under male category (3.3%).

5.3 Underemployment

In the fourth annual employment–unemployment survey an attempt has been made to estimate the level of underemployment. Based on the UPS approach, major time criterion is used to determine whether a person is employed or unemployed. Underemployment is a situation where persons are available for work and get work, albeit not to the fullest extent they seek. In the report tables are generated for those persons who are available for the entire 12 months during the reference period under the UPS approach (Table 5.3).

Table 5.3 shows that at the overall level (rural + urban) the others category constitutes the highest percentage (70%) of persons who worked for

Table 5.3 Distribution of workers aged 15 years & above available for 12 months but actually worked according to Usual Principal & Subsidiary Status Approach (PS + SS) (in %)

Particulars	*Rural*	*Urban*	*Rural + Urban*
		Scheduled Caste	
worked for 12 months	47.0	73.6	52.5
worked for 6–11 months	48.6	21.1	42.9
worked 1 to 5 months	1.4	0.6	1.2
did not get any work	3.1	4.6	3.4
		Scheduled Tribe	
worked for 12 months	44.7	70.9	48.2
worked for 6–11 months	51.0	23.8	47.4
worked 1 to 5 months	2.2	0.7	2.0
did not get any work	2.0	4.6	2.4
		Other Backward Class	
worked for 12 months	53.5	76.6	60.0
worked for 6–11 months	41.8	18.3	35.2
worked 1 to 5 months	1.4	0.4	1.1
did not get any work	3.3	4.7	3.7
		Others	
worked for 12 months	62.0	82.6	70.3
worked for 6–11 months	33.0	12.1	24.6
worked 1 to 5 months	1.1	0.4	0.8
did not get any work	3.9	4.9	

Source: Government of India, *Employment–Unemployment Scenario among Different Social Groups*, Vol. V, 2013–2014, p. 17.

12 months during the reference period, followed by 60% under the OBC category, 52% under the SC category and 48% under the ST category. In rural areas, 3.9% of persons who are available for 12 months under the others category did not get any work, followed by 3.3% under the OBC category, 3.1% under the SC category and 2.0% under the ST category. In urban areas, the proportion of persons who worked for 12 months is higher than in the rural areas. Under the others category, 82.6% persons worked for 12 months in urban areas as against 62% in rural areas. In the case of SCs, 73.6% worked for 12 months in urban areas against 47% in rural areas. While 71% in urban areas against 44.7% in rural areas worked in the case of STs. In the case of OBCs, 76.6% in urban areas and 55.5% in rural areas were in work.

5.4 Worker population rate for persons aged 15 years and above according to UPS approach (in %)

The worker population rate (WPR) is defined as the number of persons employed per 1000 persons. At the all-India level (rural + urban), the WPR is highest under the ST category with about 58%, followed by 52% under

Table 5.4 Worker population rate for persons aged 15 years & above according to the Usual Principal Status Approach (ps) (in %)

	Rural			*Urban*			*Rural + Urban*		
Particulars	*M*	*F*	*P*	*M*	*F*	*P*	*M*	*F*	*P*
SC	71.5	29.3	53.5	71.7	19.0	46.4	71.5	26.9	52.0
ST	78.1	39.3	59.7	74.2	20.7	48.1	77.6	36.7	58.1
OBC	70.6	27.9	52.3	72.3	18.0	46.0	71.1	24.8	50.5
Others	70.5	19.1	47.3	69	13.3	42.4	69.9	16.6	45.3

Source: Government of India, *Employment–Unemployment Scenario among Different Social Groups*, Vol. V, 2013–2014, p. 13.

Table 5.5 Worker population rate for persons aged 15 years & above according to Usual Principal & Subsidiary Status Approach (PS + SS) (in %)

	Rural			*Urban*			*Rural + Urban*		
Particulars	*M*	*F*	*P*	*M*	*F*	*P*	*M*	*F*	*P*
SC	74.3	38.1	58.9	72.4	20.3	47.4	73.9	34.0	56.5
ST	81.7	51.6	67.4	74.9	23.7	50.0	80.7	47.6	65.0
OBC	73.4	35.5	57.1	72.9	19.6	47.1	73.3	30.6	54.3
OTHERS	72.5	24.7	51.0	69.4	14.2	43.0	71.3	20.3	47.7

Source: Government of India, *Employment–Unemployment Scenario among Different Social Groups*, Vol. V, 2013–2014, p. 14.

the SC category, 51% for OBC and 45% for the others category, based on the UPS approach (Table 5.4). At the sectors level, i.e., rural and urban sectors, also show similar type of results as shown at (rural + urban) level. Thus, ST category is leading among all the four social groups at both (rural + urban).

The proportion of female WPR is much lower than male WPR under all the four social groups based on the UPS approach. The highest female WPR (rural + urban), of about 37%, is observed under the ST category whereas the male WPR for the same social group is about 78%, which is also highest among all the social groups. In the case of SC females, WPR is 26.9% while male WPR IS 71.5%. In the case of others, WPR is only 20% while it is 71%.

Table 5.5 shows similar trends in the UPSS approach, also as seen under the UPS approach. The ST category stands first in all the parameters i.e., national level, social group-wise, sector-wise and gender-wise.

5.5 Labour Force Participation Rate (LFPR)

The Labour Force Participation Rate (LFPR) is a measure of the proportion of a country's working age population that engages actively in the labour market, either by actually working or by actively looking for work.

Table 5.6 Labour Force Participation Rate for persons aged 15 years & above according to Usual Principal Status Approach (ps) (in %)

	Rural			*Urban*			*Rural + Urban*		
Particulars	*M*	*F*	*P*	*M*	*F*	*P*	*M*	*F*	*P*
SC	74.4	31.0	56.0	75.1	21.2	49.3	74.5	28.8	54.6
ST	81.3	41.5	62.4	77.6	22.9	50.9	80.8	38.8	60.8
OBC	73.7	29.8	54.8	75.1	20.3	48.6	74.1	26.9	53.1
OTHERS	73.8	20.8	49.9	71.7	15.6	44.9	73	18.6	47.8

Source: Government of India, *Employment–Unemployment Scenario Among Different Social Groups*, Vol. V, 2013–2014, p. 11.

It provides an indication of the size of the supply of labour available to engage in the production of goods and services.

At a national level, the LFPR (rural + urban) for the ST category is highest with 61%, followed by 55% under the SC category, 53% for the OBC category and 48% for the others category under the UPS approach. In the case of both rural and urban sectors, LFPR for the ST category is highest with about 62% in the rural sector and 51% in the urban sector, followed by the SC category (Table 5.6).

It is evident from Table 5.6 Female LFPR (rural + urban) is relatively low as compared to male LFPR. The female LFPR is highest (39%) for the ST Category among all the four social groups. For male category persons also the LFPR is highest for the ST category (81%). A similar trend is visible under the UPSS approach (Table 5.7) also where LFPR for ST category (rural + urban) is highest (66.4%), followed by 58.3% under the SC, 56% under OBC and 50% for others. In the case of the rural sector, the proportion of LFPR under the ST category is highest with about 69%, followed by 61% under the SC category, 59% under the OBC and 53% under the others category, based on the UPSS approach.

In the case of the urban sector also the proportion of LFPR under the ST category is highest with 52.4%, followed by 50% under SC, 49% under

Table 5.7 Labour Force Participation Rate for persons aged 15 years & above according to Usual Principal & Subsidiary Status Approach (in %)

	Rural			*Urban*			*Rural + Urban*		
Particulars	*M*	*F*	*P*	*M*	*F*	*P*	*M*	*F*	*P*
SC	76.3	39.1	60.5	75.3	22.3	49.9	76.1	35.3	58.3
ST	83.3	52.5	68.7	77.8	25.7	52.4	82.5	48.7	66.4
OBC	75.5	36.8	58.9	75.4	21.7	49.4	75.5	32.1	56.2
OTHERS	74.9	26.1	52.9	71.9	16.3	45.3	73.7	22.0	49.8

Source: Government of India, *Employment–Unemployment Scenario Among Different Social Groups*, Vol. I, 2013–2014, p. 12.

OBC category and 45% under the others category, based on the UPSS approach (Table 5.7). The proportion of both male and female LFPR is lowest in both rural and urban areas under the others category based on the UPSS approach. Under all of the social groups (with the exception of ST) the female LFPR is considerably lower than the male counterpart in both rural and urban areas.

5.6 Employment and unemployment situation among different social groups across the states

According to the Usual Principal & Subsidiary Status Approach (PS + SS) in 2013–2014, the unemployment is lowest among STs (rural + urban) Table 5.8 that is, at 0.3% in Gujarat, while it is highest in Jammu & Kashmir, that is, 21.4%. In the case of SCs (Table 5.9) the unemployment rate (rural + urban) is lowest in Manipur that is at 0.6% while it is highest in Nagaland, which is 21.6%. In the case of OBCs (Table 5.10) the unemployment rate is lowest in Gujarat (0.6%), while it is highest in Arunachal Pradesh (28.2%). In the case of others, the unemployment rate is lowest in Gujarat (1.2%), while it is highest in Arunachal Pradesh (18.3%).

In the case of ST Male workers (rural + urban) (Table 5.11), the unemployment rate is lowest in Gujarat, that is 0.3%, while it is highest, that is 23.3%, in Jammu & Kashmir. In the case of STs Female workers (Table 5.12) the unemployment rate is lowest (0.4%) in Gujarat while it is highest in Uttarakhand (52.4%). Unemployment among SCs male workers (Table 5.13) is lowest in Manipur (0.3%) while it is highest in Nagaland (2.3%). In the case of SCs (Table 5.14) female workers have the lowest unemployment rate in Gujarat (0.8%), while it is highest in Arunachal Pradesh (38.1%). The unemployment rate among OBCs male (Table 5.15) workers is lowest in Gujarat (0.4%) while it is highest in Nagaland (31.5%). In the case of OBCs female (Table 5.16) workers the unemployment rate is lowest in Gujarat (0.7%), while it is highest in Arunachal Pradesh (61.4%) (Table 5.17). The unemployment rate among others male workers (Table 5.18) is lowest in Assam (1.1%), while it is highest in Arunachal Pradesh (9.3%). In case of others Female workers (Table 5.19) the unemployment rate is lowest in Gujarat (2%), while it is highest in Arunachal Pradesh (36.8%).

Thus, among all states in all social groups' female workers unemployment rate is lowest in Gujarat.

Regarding unemployment in rural areas among different states, the unemployment is lowest among SCs in Gujarat (0.6%), while it is highest in Nagaland (24.8%) (Govt. of India 2013–2014, p. 105). On the other hand, the unemployment is lowest among SCs in Manipur (0.7%), while it is highest in Sikkim (28.7%) in urban areas according to Usual Principal & Subsidiary Status Approach in 2013–2014 (Govt. of India 2013–2014, p. 108)

The unemployment (rural) among STs is lowest in Telangana (0.1%), while it is highest in Jammu &Kashmir (22.8%) in rural areas (Govt. of India 2013–2014, p. 114). On the other hand, the unemployment rate is

Table 5.8 Percentage distribution of workers aged 15 years & above by Social Group available for 12 months but actually worked according to Usual Principal & Subsidiary Status Approach (PS + SS) for each State/UT. Rural + Urban (Scheduled Tribe)

Name of State/UT	*Worked for 12 months*	*Worked 6–11 months*	*Worked 1–5 months*	*Did not get any work*
Andhra Pradesh	42.5	55.4	0.1	1.9
Arunachal Pradesh	62.2	22.7	7	8.2
Assam	57.7	36.4	2.7	3.2
Bihar	49.4	45.5	0.1	4.9
Chhattisgarh	30.3	65.8	2.2	1.7
Delhi	85.8	4	2.5	7.7
Goa	82.3	6.3	4.7	6.7
Gujarat	64	35.3	0.4	0.3
Haryana	56.2	41.6	0.2	2
Himachal Pradesh	48.5	30.4	19	2.1
Jammu & Kashmir	43.7	32.9	1.9	21.4
Jharkhand	35.3	53.1	9.5	2.1
Karnataka	55	42.3	0.6	2.1
Kerala	49	44.7	-	6.2
Madhya Pradesh	51.5	46.5	0.6	1.3
Maharashtra	43.3	54.3	0.4	2
Manipur	36.8	56.5	0.1	6.5
Meghalaya	54.7	42.3	0.5	2.5
Mizoram	56.5	39.9	1.3	2.2
Nagaland	59.2	31	3.1	6.7
Odisha	27.4	67.1	2.9	2.6
Punjab	86	12.2	-	1.8
Rajasthan	49.2	42.2	5.7	2.9
Sikkim	58.9	30.1	0.2	10.8
Tamil Nadu	73.5	25.4	-	1.1
Telangana	49.8	49.6	-	0.6
Tripura	30.3	56.8	8.5	4.4
Uttarakhand	55.4	28.4	0.2	15.9
Uttar Pradesh	46.9	47.3	1.2	4.6
West Bengal	54.1	41.9	1.5	2.5
Chandigarh	95.8	4.2	-	-
Dagra & Nagar Haveli	70.2	28.2	-	1.5
Diu & Daman	&	Diu	77.4	22.6
Lakshadweep	61.6	22.4	0.5	15.5
Puducherry	-	-	-	-
India	48.2	47.4	2	2.4

Sources: "Employment–Unemployment Scenario among different Social Groups 2013–2014", Government of India, Ministry of Labour & Employment Labour Bureau, Chandigarh, p. 97.

lowest among STs in Andhra Pradesh that is at 0.9%, while it is highest in Kerala (51.7%) in urban areas according to the Usual Principal & Subsidiary Status Approach in 2013–2014 (Govt. of India 2013–2014, p. 117).

The unemployment is lowest among OBCs in Gujarat (0.4%), while it is highest in Arunachal Pradesh (55.5%) in rural areas (Govt. of India

Table 5.9 Percentage distribution of workers aged 15 years & above by Social Group available for 12 months but actually worked according to Usual Principal & Subsidiary Status Approach (PS + SS) for each State/UT. Rural + Urban (Scheduled Caste)

Name of State/UT	*Worked for 12 months*	*Worked 6–11 months*	*Worked 1–5 months*	*Did not get any work*
Andhra Pradesh	53.8	40.5	0.8	5
Arunachal Pradesh	72.8	12.7	-	14.4
Assam	67.6	27.2	2.3	2.9
Bihar	32.7	63	1	3.3
Chhattisgarh	39.9	57.4	0.7	2
Delhi	90.2	5.7	0.5	3.7
Goa	95.1	-	-	4.9
Gujarat	62.5	36.4	0.4	0.7
Haryana	52.5	41.6	3.1	2.9
Himachal Pradesh	66.9	31.1	1.3	0.7
Jammu & Kashmir	51.5	35.9	1.9	10.8
Jharkhand	34.5	54.8	8.2	2.6
Karnataka	66.5	32.2	0.1	1.2
Kerala	50.7	38	1.7	9.6
Madhya Pradesh	52.5	45.6	0.3	1.6
Maharashtra	57.1	39.7	0.7	2.5
Manipur	54.7	37.9	6.7	0.6
Meghalaya	100	-	-	-
Mizoram	42.1	40.2	10.9	6.8
Nagaland	59.6	17.7	1.1	21.6
Odisha	40.5	54.3	1.6	3.6
Punjab	68.2	26.2	0.3	5.3
Rajasthan	51.6	42	3.2	3.1
Sikkim	47.3	50.9	-	1.7
Tamil Nadu	65.9	29.9	0.1	4.1
Telangana	46.4	51.8	0.1	1.7
Tripura	32.2	56.5	2.1	9.1
Uttarakhand	49.8	38	5.2	6.9
Uttar Pradesh	41.6	52.4	2.3	3.7
West Bengal	60.5	34.8	0.6	4.1
India	52.5	42.9	1.2	3.4

Sources: "Employment–Unemployment Scenario among different Social Groups 2013–2014", Government of India, Ministry of Labour & Employment Labour Bureau, Chandigarh", p. 102.

2013–2014, p. 126). On the other hand, the unemployment rate is lowest among OBCs in Gujarat (1.1%), while it is highest in Nagaland (24%) in urban areas, according to the Usual Principal & Subsidiary Status Approach in 2013–2014. The unemployment is lowest among others in Tamil Nadu (0.6%), while it is highest in Arunachal Pradesh (34.6%), followed by Mizoram (33.3%) in rural areas (Govt. of India 2013–2014, p. 132). On the other hand, the unemployment is lowest among others in Gujarat (0.4%), followed by Goa (10.3%), while it is highest in Sikkim (18.7%), according

Table 5.10 Percentage distribution of workers aged 15 years & above by Social Group available for 12 months but actually worked according to Usual Principal & Subsidiary Status Approach (PS + SS) for each State/UT. Rural + Urban (Other Backward Class)

Name of the state/UT	*Worked for 12 months*	*Worked 6–11 months*	*Worked 1–5 months*	*Did not get any work*
Andhra Pradesh	57	39.9	0.4	2.7
Arunachal Pradesh	59.4	12.3	-	28.2
Assam	63.8	28.5	3	4.7
Bihar	47.9	45.2	0.8	6.1
Chhattisgarh	39.2	56.2	2.4	2.2
Delhi	91.5	2.7	1.1	4.7
Goa	79.7	1.4	1.3	17.7
Gujarat	78.7	20.1	0.5	0.6
Haryana	75.2	21.9	1.4	1.5
Himachal Pradesh	60.2	33.7	4.1	2
Jammu Kashmir	56	31.6	0.2	12.3
Jharkhand	48.1	42.5	6.2	3.2
Karnataka	70.4	27.4	0.1	2.1
Kerala	64.4	24.5	1.5	9.6
Madhya Pradesh	59.6	37.5	0.3	2.7
Maharashtra	60.8	36.6	0.4	2.3
Manipur	65.8	27.4	3.6	3.2
Meghalaya	75.1	2.3	22.7	-
Mizoram	50.8	40.7	-	8.5
Nagaland	76	-	-	24
Odisha	36.3	56.1	1.3	6.3
Punjab	78	16.6	0.3	5.1
Rajasthan	59.1	35.4	2.4	3.2
Sikkim	75.6	20.4	-	4
Tamil Nadu	76.1	20.1	0.3	3.6
Telangana	47.5	49	0.1	3.4
Tripura	47	34.6	5.9	12.6
Uttarakhand	79.4	17.3	1.8	1.6
Uttar Pradesh	50.9	42.8	2	4.3
West Bengal	68.6	26.1	2.6	2.7
Islands	69.9	19.2	2	8.9
India	60	35.2	1.1	3.7

Sources: "Employment–Unemployment Scenario among different Social Groups 2013–2014", Government of India, Ministry of Labour& Employment Labour Bureau, Chandigarh, p. 120.

to the Usual Principal & Subsidiary Status Approach in 2013–2014 (Govt. of India 2013–2014, p. 135).

5.7 Conclusion

Based on the UPS approach, the unemployment rate at the all-India level (rural + urban) is 5.3% under the others category, which is the highest recorded among all four social groups. In the case of OBC, the unemployment

Table 5.11 Percentage distribution of workers aged 15 years & above by social group available for 12 months but actually worked according to Usual Principal & Subsidiary Status Approach (PS + SS) for each State/UT. Rural + Urban (Scheduled Tribe) Male

Name of the State/UT	*Worked for 12 months*	*Worked 6–11 months*	*Worked 1–5 months*	*Did not get any work*
Andhra Pradesh	49.1	48.8	-	2.1
Arunachal Pradesh	62.4	23.9	6	7.7
Assam	57.1	38.3	2.6	2
Bihar	54	40.6	0.2	5.3
Chhattisgarh	32.2	64.6	1.7	1.5
Delhi	87.3	4.4	1	7.3
Goa	82.9	8.3	6.2	2.6
Gujarat	67.9	31.5	0.3	0.3
Haryana	54.3	43.2	0.2	2.3
Himachal Pradesh	52.5	25.8	20.5	1.3
Jammu & Kashmir	41.7	34	1	23.3
Jharkhand	35.7	54.7	7.9	1.7
Karnataka	59.6	39.3	0.3	0.8
Kerala	58.7	41.1	-	0.2
Madhya Pradesh	51.3	46.5	0.6	1.5
Maharashtra	47.7	49.4	0.5	2.3
Manipur	40.2	55.7	0.2	3.9
Meghalaya	53.2	43.3	0.7	2.7
Mizoram	54.7	41.9	1.6	1.7
Nagaland	58.6	33.9	1.4	6.1
Odisha	30.6	65.8	1.7	1.9
Punjab	85.8	12.4	-	1.8
Rajasthan	50.2	43.4	3	3.4
Sikkim	55.9	37.5	-	6.7
Tamil Nadu	78.5	20.8	-	0.8
Telangana	52.9	46.4	-	0.7
Tripura	31.3	63.1	5	0.6
Uttarakhand	67.8	27.5	-	4.7
Uttar Pradesh	46.9	47.6	1.2	4.2
West Bengal	57.1	38.4	2	2.4
Lakshadweep	65.3	23.7	0.7	10.2
All India	**50.4**	**45.7**	**1.7**	**2.2**

Sources: "Employment–Unemployment Scenario among different Social Groups 2013–2014", Government of India, Ministry of Labour & Employment Labour Bureau, Chandigarh, p. 112.

rate is estimated to be 4.8%, followed by 4.6% under the SC category and the lowest is 4.5% under the ST category in 2013–2014. In the case of rural areas, the ST category has the lowest unemployment rate, i.e., 4.3%, whereas it is highest in the others category (5.3%). In urban areas, the unemployment rate is lowest (5.3%) under the OBC category, while it is the highest in the case of the SC Category (5.8%).

While comparing the gender-wise unemployment rate (Rural + Urban) at the all-India level under the UPS approach there is a wide variation between

Table 5.12 Percentage distribution of workers aged 15 years & above by social group available for 12 months but actually worked according to Usual Principal & Subsidiary Status Approach (PS + SS) for each State/UT. Rural + Urban (Scheduled Tribe) Female

Name of State/UT	*Worked for 12 months*	*Worked for 6–11 months*	*Worked for 1–5 months*	*Did not get any work*
Andhra Pradesh	32.7	65.4	0.2	1.7
Arunachal Pradesh	61.8	21.1	8.3	8.8
Assam	60	29	3	8
Bihar	12.1	85.8	-	2.1
Chhattisgarh	27.1	67.9	2.9	2.1
Delhi	71.7		17	11.3
Goa	80.7	-	-	19.3
Gujarat	55.4	43.6	0.6	0.4
Haryana	70	30	-	-
Himachal Pradesh	38.6	41.6	15.6	4.2
Jammu & Kashmir	52.3	28.3	6.2	13.2
Jharkhand	32.8	41.1	21	5.1
Karnataka	44.7	49	1.4	4.8
Kerala	35.6	49.9	-	14.6
Madhya Pradesh	51.9	46.6	0.7	0.8
Maharashtra	33.2	65.4	0.2	1.3
Manipur	27.4	58.8	-	13.8
Meghalaya	56.9	40.8	0.1	2.2
Mizoram	59.3	36.8	0.9	3
Nagaland	60.7	23.7	7.4	8.1
Odisha	17.7	71.1	6.2	5
Punjab	100	-	-	-
Rajasthan	47.1	39.5	11.8	1.6
Sikkim	65.6	13.2	0.7	20.5
Tamil Nadu	62.4	35.8	-	1.8
Telangana	45.6	53.9	-	0.5
Tripura	26	29.3	23.5	21.1
Uttarakhand	15.3	31.5	0.8	52.4
Uttar Pradesh	46.3	41.6	-	12.1
West Bengal	45.3	51.9	0.1	2.7
Puducherry	-	-	-	-
All India	**42.9**	**51.5**	**2.9**	**2.8**

Sources: "Employment–Unemployment Scenario among different Social Groups 2013–2014", Government of India, Ministry of Labour & Employment Labour Bureau, Chandigarh, p. 113.

the male and female unemployment rates. In the case of females, the maximum unemployment rate is estimated to be 10.5% under the others category whereas for males the unemployment rate is 4.2% in the same social group. In urban areas, the unemployment rate among females is highest (14.5%) in the case of others, while it is the lowest in the case of ST females (9.5%) and in the case of SC females it is 10.7%.

The female unemployment rate (Rural + Urban) at the all-India level is higher than the male unemployment rate across all the four social groups,

Table 5.13 Percentage distribution of workers aged 15 years & above by Social Group available for 12 months but actually worked according to Usual Principal & Subsidiary Status Approach (PS + SS) for each State/UT. Rural + Urban (Scheduled Caste) Male

Name of the State/UT	*Worked for 12 months*	*Worked 6-11 months*	*Worked 1 to 5 months*	*Did not get any work*
Andhra Pradesh	60.5	33.9	0.8	4.8
Arunachal Pradesh	95.3	1.2	-	3.5
Assam	68.7	28.1	1.6	1.6
Bihar	34.7	61.4	0.8	3
Chhattisgarh	45.4	52.1	0.7	1.8
Delhi	91.5	4.9	0.5	3.1
Goa	92.5	-	-	7.5
Gujarat	65.9	33.2	0.2	0.7
Haryana	53.8	41.5	2.2	2.5
Himachal Pradesh	59.1	39.7	0.4	0.8
Jammu Kashmir	52	35.2	2.1	10.7
Jharkhand	35.1	56.1	6.8	2.1
Karnataka	68.6	30	0.2	1.2
Kerala	53	41.8	-	5.2
Madhya Pradesh	56	41.8	0.3	1.8
Maharashtra	61.9	35.2	0.5	2.4
Manipur	53.3	34.7	11.7	0.3
Meghalaya	100	-	-	-
Mizoram	50.9	39.9	7.2	2
Nagaland	54.8	23.5	1.5	20.3
Odisha	42.3	53.4	1.2	3.1
Punjab	69.4	27.2	0.2	3.2
Rajasthan	53.8	42.6	0.7	3
Sikkim	55.1	43.7	-	1.2
Tamil Nadu	67.9	27.7	0.1	4.3
Telangana	50.6	47.9	0.2	1.4
Tripura	30.2	64.3	-	5.5
Uttarakhand	55.7	32.4	5.6	6.2
Uttar Pradesh	41.6	53.2	2.1	3.2
West Bengal	62.3	33.1	0.7	3.9
Puducherry	62.2	12.9	-	24.9
All India	54	41.9	1	3

Sources: "Employment–Unemployment Scenario among different Social Groups 2013–2014", Government of India, Ministry of Labour & Employment Labour Bureau, Chandigarh, p. 103.

with the exception of ST. Under the ST category, the female unemployment rate is 2.1%, whereas under the male category it is 2.2%. In the case of others, the female unemployment rate is more than double (7.8%) that recorded for males (3.3%).

With reference to underemployment, under the UP & SS approach (Rural + Urban) in the others category the highest percentage (70%) of persons worked for 12 months during the reference period. This was followed by

Table 5.14 Percentage distribution of workers aged 15 years & above by social group available for 12 months but actually worked according to Usual Principal & Subsidiary Status Approach (PS + SS) for each State/UT. Rural + Urban (Scheduled Caste) Female

Name of the State/UT	*Worked for 12 months*	*Worked 6–11 months*	*Worked 1 to 5 months*	*Did not get any work*
Andhra Pradesh	43	51.1	0.7	5.2
Arunachal Pradesh	24.1	37.7	-	38.1
Assam	62.8	22.7	5.8	8.8
Bihar	24.9	68.9	1.9	4.3
Chhattisgarh	29.8	67.2	0.7	2.3
Delhi	79.3	12	-	8.8
Goa	100	-	-	-
Gujarat	49.3	48.7	1.3	0.8
Haryana	44.4	41.8	8.3	5.6
Himachal Pradesh	80	16.7	2.8	0.5
Jammu & Kashmir	46.5	42.2	-	11.2
Jharkhand	28.4	42.2	21.9	7.5
Karnataka	62.1	36.6	-	1.3
Kerala	47	31.8	4.4	16.8
Madhya Pradesh	42.7	56.1	0.2	1.1
Maharashtra	46	50.3	1.1	2.6
Manipur	56.7	42.3	-	1
Meghalaya	100	-	-	-
Mizoram	2.3	41.6	27.7	28.4
Nagaland	74.4	-	-	25.6
Odisha	32.7	58.2	3.3	5.8
Punjab	60.4	19.9	1	18.7
Rajasthan	43.4	39.7	13.1	3.7
Sikkim	12	84	-	4
Tamil Nadu	62	34.3	0.1	3.7
Telangana	40.3	57.3	0.1	2.3
Tripura	40.4	26.4	10.4	22.9
Uttarakhand	28	58.9	3.7	9.4
Uttar Pradesh	42.8	39.2	5.6	12.4
West Bengal	50.1	44.3	0.4	5.2
All India	47	46.5	1.9	4.6

Sources: "Employment–Unemployment Scenario among different Social Groups 2013–14", Government of India, Ministry of Labour& Employment Labour Bureau, Chandigarh, p. 104.

60% under the OBC category, 52% under the SC category and 48% under the ST category. In rural areas, 3.9% of persons who are available for 12 months under the others category got no work, followed by 3.3% under the OBC category, 3.1% under the SC category and 2.0% under the ST category. For all categories, the proportion of persons who worked for 12 months is higher in urban areas than in rural areas.

At the all-India level the LFPR (Rural + Urban) for the ST category is highest, at 61%, followed by 55% under the SC category, 53% for the OBC

Table 5.15 Percentage distribution of workers aged 15 years & above by Social Group available for 12 months but actually worked according to Usual Principal & Subsidiary Status Approach (PS + SS) for each State/UT. Rural +Urban (Other Backward Class) Male

Name of the State/UT	*Worked for 12 months*	*Worked 6–11 months*	*Worked 1 to 5 months*	*Did not get any work*
Andhra Pradesh	64.5	32.4	0.5	2.6
Arunachal Pradesh	66.9	16.8	-	16.4
Assam	67.1	28.5	2.1	2.4
Bihar	49.2	44.6	0.7	5.5
Chhattisgarh	44.3	51.7	1.6	2.4
Delhi	93.4	2	0.6	4
Goa	79.6	1.1	1.6	17.7
Gujarat	82.5	16.7	0.2	0.6
Haryana	75.5	22	1.2	1.3
Himachal Pradesh	64.7	31.4	3.3	0.6
Jammu Kashmir	56.9	36	0.2	6.8
Jharkhand	49.1	42.9	6	2
Karnataka	75.1	23.1	0	1.8
Kerala	70.1	24.8	1	4.1
Madhya Pradesh	60.9	36.5	0.3	2.3
Maharashtra	66.5	30.9	0.3	2.2
Manipur	70.3	23.5	3.5	2.7
Meghalaya	75.1	2.3	22.7	-
Mizoram	67.7	32.3	-	-
Nagaland	68.5	-	-	31.5
Odisha	39.9	53.7	1.1	5.3
Punjab	78.8	17.2	0.2	3.8
Rajasthan	60.6	34.9	1.5	3
Sikkim	75.6	19.9	-	4.5
Tamil Nadu	78.6	18.9	0.2	2.4
Telangana	55.6	41.5	0.2	2.8
Tripura	49.7	36.6	1.2	12.5
Uttarakhand	82.8	15.2	0.7	1.4
Uttar Pradesh	51.8	42.9	1.9	3.5
West Bengal	69.9	25.4	2.6	2.1
India	62.5	33.5	1	3

Sources: "Employment–Unemployment Scenario among Different Social Groups 2013–2014", Government of India, Ministry of Labour & Employment Labour Bureau, Chandigarh, p. 121.

category and 48% for the others category under the UPS approach. In the case of the rural sector and also in the urban sector the LFPR for the ST category is highest, with about 62% and 51%, respectively, followed by the SC category with56% in the rural sector and 49.3% in the urban sector.

According to the Usual Principal & Subsidiary Status Approach (PS + SS) in 2013–2014 regarding unemployment among different states, the unemployment rate (Rural + Urban) is the lowest among STs in Gujarat (0.3%),

Table 5.16 Percentage distribution of workers aged 15 years & above by social group available for 12 months but actually worked according to Usual Principal & Subsidiary Status Approach (PS+SS) for each State/UT. Rural +Urban (Other Backward Class) Female

Name of the State/UT	*Worked for 12 months*	*Worked 6–11 months*	*Worked 1 to 5 months*	*Did not get any work*
Andhra Pradesh	43.4	53.5	0.1	3
Arunachal Pradesh	38.6	-	-	61.4
Assam	52.9	28.3	6.2	12.6
Bihar	37.8	49.8	1.6	10.7
Chhattisgarh	30	64.4	3.7	1.9
Delhi	76.1	8.1	5.3	10.5
Goa	79.9	2.5	-	17.6
Gujarat	63.9	33.9	1.5	0.7
Haryana	73.2	21.4	2.7	2.7
Himachal Pradesh	46.9	40.5	6.5	6.1
Jammu & Kashmir	51.9	11.6	-	36.4
Jharkhand	40.4	39.5	7.9	12.2
Karnataka	58	38.7	0.2	3
Kerala	50.6	23.7	2.7	23
Madhya Pradesh	54.1	41.6	0.2	4
Maharashtra	45.8	51.3	0.6	2.4
Manipur	56.7	35.4	3.7	4.2
Meghalaya	-	-	-	-
Mizoram	11.1	60.5	-	28.4
Nagaland	100	-	-	-
Odisha	19.4	67.2	2.4	10.9
Punjab	70.3	10.5	1	18.2
Rajasthan	51.4	37.7	7.1	3.8
Sikkim	75.1	24.9	-	-
Tamil Nadu	70	23.1	0.4	6.5
Telangana	34.9	60.7	0	4.4
Tripura	37.6	27.6	21.9	13
Uttarakhand	61.4	28.3	7.4	2.9
Uttar Pradesh	36.1	41	4.5	18.4
West Bengal	62.2	29.6	2.7	5.5
Islands	72	12.4	-	15.6
Puducherry	83.7	10.9	-	5.4
India	50.5	41.6	1.6	6.3

Sources: "Employment–Unemployment Scenario among different Social Groups 2013–2014", Government of India, Ministry of Labour & Employment Labour Bureau, Chandigarh, p. 122.

while it is highest in Jammu & Kashmir (21.4%). In the case of SCs, the unemployment rate (Rural + Urban) is lowest in Manipur (0.6%), while it is highest in Nagaland (21.6%). In the case of OBCs, the unemployment rate is lowest in Gujarat (0.6%), while it is highest in Arunachal Pradesh (28.2%). In the case of others, the unemployment rate is lowest in Gujarat (1.2%), while it is highest in Arunachal Pradesh (18.3%).

Table 5.17 Percentage distribution of workers aged 15 years & above by social group available for 12 months but actually worked according to Usual Principal & Subsidiary Status Approach (PS + SS) for each State/UT (Rural +Urban (Others))

Name of State/UT	*Worked for 12 months*	*Worked 6–11 months*	*Worked 1–5 months*	*Did not get any work*
Andhra Pradesh	69	26.6	0.6	3.8
Arunachal Pradesh	75	5	1.8	18.3
Assam	71.6	24.6	1.7	2.1
Bihar	51.2	40.4	0.4	8
Chhattisgarh	75.4	18.7	0.6	5.3
Delhi	92.6	2.5	0.6	4.3
Goa	84.9	4.8	-	10.2
Gujarat	87.2	11.4	0.2	1.2
Haryana	75.3	20	1	3.7
Himachal Pradesh	75.7	17.4	4.3	2.6
Jammu Kashmir	65.2	26	0.6	8.3
Jharkhand	59.3	34.9	2	3.7
Karnataka	67.4	31.2	0	1.4
Kerala	71.7	16.2	1	11
Madhya Pradesh	71.2	24.9	0.2	3.7
Maharashtra	75.6	21.9	0.5	2
Manipur	22.2	63.1	12.9	1.8
Meghalaya	61.9	30.9	3	4.2
Mizoram	95.1	-	-	4.9
Nagaland	69.4	23.3	2.4	4.8
Odisha	61.6	32.7	0.7	5.1
Punjab	80.8	12.6	0.5	6.1
Rajasthan	64.6	29.2	1.2	5
Sikkim	60.4	21.2	5.8	12.6
Tamil Nadu	81.2	16	-	2.8
Telangana	74.8	17.9	0	7.2
Tripura	59	33.9	1.6	5.4
Uttarakhand	66	25	1.7	7.4
Uttar Pradesh	60.6	31.3	2	6.2
West Bengal	70.5	24.6	0.5	4.3
India	70.3	24.6	0.8	4.3

Source: Government of India, Ministry of Labour & Employment Labour Bureau, Chandigarh. "Employment–Unemployment Scenario among different Social Groups 2013–2014, p. 129.

Table 5.18 Percentage distribution of workers aged 15 years & above by social group available for 12 months but actually worked according to Usual Principal & Subsidiary Status Approach (PS + SS) for each State/UT (Rural +Urban (Others)) (Male)

Name of the State/UT	*Worked for 12 months*	*Worked 6–11 months*	*Worked 1–5 months*	*Did not get any work*
Andhra Pradesh	74.7	22.5	0.4	2.3
Arunachal Pradesh	86.8	2.3	1.6	9.3
Assam	74	23.7	1.2	1.1
Bihar	52.3	40.5	0.3	6.9
Chhattisgarh	77.6	17.1	0.6	4.7
Delhi	94.2	2.1	0.1	3.5
Goa	89.6	4.5	-	5.8
Gujarat	88.5	10.3	0.1	1.1
Haryana	75	20.7	1	3.2
Himachal Pradesh	74.2	19.3	3.7	2.9
Jammu & Kashmir	65.7	28.2	0.4	5.6
Jharkhand	58.4	36.4	2	3.3
Karnataka	68.9	29.9	0	1.2
Kerala	78.1	18.1	0.8	3
Madhya Pradesh	73.1	23	0.3	3.6
Maharashtra	78.5	19.3	0.4	1.8
Manipur	21.2	69	9.1	0.7
Meghalaya	62.3	34.9	2.1	0.6
Mizoram	92.5	-	-	7.5
Nagaland	66.8	26.3	2.7	4.2
Odisha	61.9	33.8	0.6	3.7
Punjab	81.8	13.4	0.5	4.3
Rajasthan	66.7	28.2	1.1	4
Sikkim	68.2	22.3	2.8	6.7
Tamil Nadu	83	14.6	-	2.3
Telangana	81.1	15.9	0	2.9
Tripura	65.7	30.8	0.4	3.2
Uttarakhand	71.1	20.8	1.9	6.2
Uttar Pradesh	60.8	32.2	2	5.1
West Bengal	71.8	24.6	0.5	3.1
Puducherry	79.1	2.2	-	18.7
All India	71.8	24.2	0.8	3.2

Sources: "Employment–Unemployment Scenario among different Social Groups 2013–14", Government of India, Ministry of Labour & Employment Labour Bureau, Chandigarh, p. 130.

Table 5.19 Percentage distribution of workers aged 15 years & above by Social Group available for 12 months but actually worked according to Usual Principal & Subsidiary Status Approach (PS + SS) for each State/UT (Rural +Urban (Others)) (Female)

Name of the State/UT	*Worked for 12 months*	*Worked 6–11 months*	*Worked 1–5 months*	*Did not get any work*
Andhra Pradesh	54.5	37	0.9	7.6
Arunachal Pradesh	50.7	10.4	2.1	36.8
Assam	58.2	29.8	4.6	7.4
Bihar	41.1	39.2	2.2	17.6
Chhattisgarh	66.7	24.7	0.9	7.7
Delhi	80.5	5.2	4.2	10.1
Goa	71.3	5.6	-	23.1
Gujarat	79.9	17.5	0.6	2
Haryana	77.9	14	0.9	7.1
Himachal Pradesh	78.3	14.2	5.4	2.1
Jammu & Kashmir	62.1	14	1.3	22.6
Jharkhand	70.4	18.8	2.6	8.2
Karnataka	62.5	35.3	0	2.2
Kerala	58	12.2	1.4	28.3
Madhya Pradesh	60.9	34.8	-	4.3
Maharashtra	67.2	29.7	0.6	2.5
Manipur	24.9	47.1	23.1	4.9
Meghalaya	60.7	18.7	5.6	15.1
Mizoram	100	-	-	-
Nagaland	90.3	-	-	9.7
Odisha	58.5	21.8	1.7	17.9
Punjab	73.2	6.6	0.3	19.9
Rajasthan	53.4	34.6	1.7	10.3
Sikkim	32.5	17.1	16.5	33.9
Tamil Nadu	74.5	21	-	4.5
Telangana	58.7	22.9	-	18.4
Tripura	36.5	44.4	6	13.1
Uttarakhand	49.8	38.1	1.1	11
Uttar Pradesh	57.8	19.1	1.9	21.2
West Bengal	62.4	24.9	0.4	12.3
All India	63.1	26.6	1.1	9.2

Sources: "Employment–Unemployment Scenario among different Social Groups 2013–2014", Government of India, Ministry of Labour & Employment Labour Bureau, Chandigarh, p. 131.

Notes

1 **Usual activity status:** The usual activity status relates to the activity status of a person during the last completed twelve months from the date of survey. The activity in which a person spent relatively longer time (major time criterion) during the reference period is considered as the usual principal activity of the person (Govt. of India, 2013–2014, *Employment–Unemployment Scenario Among Different Social Groups*, Vol. V, pp. 6–7).

2 **Subsidiary economic activity status:** A person whose usual principal status is determined on the basis of the major time criterion may have pursued some other economic activity for 30 days or more during the reference period. The status in which such economic activity is pursued during the reference period is the subsidiary economic activity status. In multiple subsidiary economic activities, subsidiary activity will be determined on the basis of relatively longer time spent criterion (Govt. of India, 2013–2014, *Employment– Unemployment Scenario Among Different Social Groups*, Vol. V, p. 7).

Reference

Government of India, Ministry of Labour and Employment. (2013–2014). *Employment–Unemployment Scenario Among Different Social Groups*. Labour Bureau, Chandigarh.

6 Caste, land and human rights of Dalits

A perspective

6.1 Introduction

Dalits were subject to a social stigma called 'untouchability'. They were denied a right to education and the right to owning land. They were also denied the right to wage bargaining and they should accept whatever was paid to them. They had to perform a number of duties in villages without any remuneration. Ambedkar observed that untouchability was not only a system of social discrimination against Dalits, but also a system of uncontrolled and unmitigated economic exploitation (Government of Maharashtra, 1989, Vol. 5, p. 94). Dalits who have been subject to deprivation and economic exploitation for centuries remained socially and economically weak even after 70 years of Independence. They are not in a position to exercise their basic human rights despite constitutional safeguards as more than 60% of Dalits workers remained as agricultural workers, mostly, landless labourers and suffering from acute poverty.

An attempt is made in this chapter to examine the change in the structure of the workforce with reference to Scheduled Castes agricultural workers at the micro level during 1964–1994 and at the national level from 1971–2011 in the context of agricultural growth to understand the linkages between caste, land and the violation of human rights in the case of Dalits and their dependence on agriculture as landless labourers. Census data and NSSO data are utilised to analyse changes in the structure of the Scheduled Caste workforce and their access to land at the national level. Two village studies were utilised for understanding the change at the micro level.

6.2 Change in the Scheduled Caste work force structure

In 1971, Scheduled Castes (Table 6.1) constituted 14.83% of the all-India population, of which 88.06% lived in rural areas and 11.94% lived in urban areas. In Andhra Pradesh, they constituted 13.37% of the total population (Table 6.2), of which 88.18% lived in a rural area and 11.28% lived in urban areas. According to the 1981 Census, the Scheduled Castes

DOI: 10.4324/9781003147053-6

Table 6.1 Rural and Urban population among different social groups in India (1971–2011)

	SC			*General*	
Year	*Rural*	*Urban*	*As % of total population*	*Rural*	*Urban*
1971	88.06	11.94	14.83	77.16	22.84
1981	84.0	16.0	14.75	-	-
1991	81.28	19.72	16.48	74.27	29.23
2001	79.82	17.18	16.2	70.17	31.6
2011	76.0	24.0	16.6	64.73	35.27

Source: 1. Census of India, 1981, Series 1, Paper – I, Union Primary Census Abstract for Scheduled Castes/Scheduled Tribes, pp. xxiii–xxv.

2. Census of India, 1991, Series 1, Paper – I, Union Primary Census Abstract for Scheduled Castes/Scheduled Tribes, p. 3.

3. Primary Census Abstract for Total population, Scheduled Castes and Scheduled Tribes, 2011 Office of the Registrar General & Census Commissioner, India.

Table 6.2 Rural and Urban population among different social groups in Andhra Pradesh (1971–2011)

	SC			*General Others*	
Years	*Rural*	*Urban*	*As % of total population*	*Rural*	*Urban*
1971	88.18	11.82	13.37	78.83	21.17
1981	84.81	15.19	14.75	73.87	26.13
1991	82.69	17.30	15.93	69.46	30.54
2001	82.82	17.18	16.2	68.88	31.12
2011	80.0	20.0	16.4	59.40	40.60

Source: Various Reports of Statistical Abstract, Government of Andhra Pradesh.

constituted 14.75% of the total population at the all-India level. Of the total Scheduled Castes population, 84% lived in rural areas and the remaining 16% in urban areas. In Andhra Pradesh, Scheduled Castes constituted 14.8% of the total population. Of the total SC population, 84.81% lived in rural areas and 15.19% in urban areas.

From Table 6.1, according to the 1991 Census, the Scheduled Castes population constituted 16.48% of total population at the all-India level. Out of the total SC population, 81.28% cent lived in rural areas and 18.72% lived in urban areas. In the case of Andhra Pradesh, Scheduled Castes constituted 15.93% of the total population, of which 82.69% rural and 17.30% urban, while in the case of the general population 69.46% lived in rural areas and 30.54% lived in urban areas. According to the 2001 Census, SC constituted 16.2% of total population at the all-India level. Of the total population of SCs,79.82% lived in rural areas while 20.18% lived in urban areas. In the case of Andhra Pradesh, SC constituted 16.2% of the total population in 2001. Out of the total SC population, 82.82% lived in rural areas while 17.18% lived in urban areas.

According to the2011 Census, SCs constituted 16.6% of the total population at the all-India level. Out of the total SC population, 76% lived in rural areas and 24% lived in urban areas while in the case of the general population 64.73% lived in rural areas and 35.27% lived in urban areas. From Table 6.2, in the case of AP, SCs population constituted 16.4% of total population, of which 80% lived in rural areas and 20% lived in urban areas while in the case of the general population 59.40% lived in rural areas and 40.60% lived in urban areas.

It is to be noted from Chapter 3, Table 3.5 that the percentage of cultivators declined in all categories, while it is very significant in the case of SCs. During 2001–2011 in the case of SC cultivators it declined from 26.78% to 14.80%, while it remained almost same (at 46%) in the case of SC agricultural labourers in 2011. Thus, most of the SC agricultural workers were agricultural labourers in 2011 at the all-India level. It is also to be noted that as per NSSO Report (No. 571, 70th round, Jan.–Dec. 2013, p. 28; Chapter 3, Table 3.1) the SCs rural households constitute more than 20% of total rural households but control only 8.52% of area owned, while others households (Non SC/ST/OBC) constitute 23.23% of total rural households, but control more than 32% of total area owned in 2013. This shows clearly that SCs have very low levels of access to land.

In Andhra Pradesh SCs cultivators (Table 6.3) constituted 12.77% of SCs main workers while SCs agricultural labourers constituted 72% in 1991. Thus, 84% of SCs workers depends on agriculture in Andhra Pradesh, with most of them as agricultural labourers in 1991, while 75% of SCs main workers depended on agriculture at the all-India level. In 2011, SC cultivators constituted 7.94% while agricultural labourers constituted 64.35% of SC main workers. That is, 72.29% of SC main workers depends on agriculture (mostly as agricultural labourers) in 2011.

Table 6.3 Occupational distribution in Andhra Pradesh

	Percentage in Total Main workers of SCs				*Percentage in Total Main workers general population*			
Category	*1971*	*1981*	*2001*	*2011*	*1971*	*1981*	*2001*	*2011*
Cultivators	14.66	17.41	11.59	7.94	32.45	32.73	25.47	18.42
Agricultural Labourers	73.04	68.24	64.21	64.35	38.24	36.78	33.83	39.96
Non-farming workers	12.3	14.35	24.20	27.71	29.31	30.49	40.30	41.62

Source: Statistical Abstract of Andhra Pradesh, 1971, 1981, 1991, 2001 and 2011.

6.3 Change in the structure of Scheduled Caste workforce at village level

In view of the high percentage of SCs living in rural areas and also about 50% of their workers are agricultural labourers, an attempt is made to study the position of SC agricultural labourers vis-à-vis others and the changing composition of SC agricultural labourers, in the context of the Green Revolution and various developmental measures undertaken by the government since 1971, at the village level.

This chapter examines at the micro-level, i.e. in two villages: (a) the position of the Scheduled Castes as agricultural labourers vis-à-vis the others; and (b) the changing proportion of Scheduled Castes permanent farm servants (Palerulu) in the total Scheduled Castes agricultural labourers and the important reasons for this change. Two Deltaic villages, Kanchakoduru in Krishna District and Malkapalli in West Godavari District in Andhra Pradesh, have been selected on the following grounds: They each have a significant proportion of Scheduled Castes and exposed to the Green Revolution and various developmental measures initiated by the government, like land reforms and others relating to a direct attack on poverty. In the case of Kanchakoduru village, the analysis covers the period up to 1982 and the position and change in the composition of Scheduled Castes labourers could be presented up to 1982 only. This has been drawn from my work published in *Social Action* (Nancharaiah, 1990, pp. 172–183). From this study it follows that by 1981–1982 most of the Palerulu gave up that job of permanent farm servants (Palerulu) and became casual labourers. Thus, they predominantly remained as agricultural labourers. However, inequalities in the distribution of land persisted despite state intervention in the form of land reform. It has been found that in 1982 holdings below five acres constituted 88% of total holdings, but controlled only 52% of total land owned. On the other hand, holdings above 10 acres constituted only 4% of total holdings but controlled 26% of the total land owned.

6.4 Malkapalli

In case of the other village, Malkapalli, the analysis covers the period up to 1994. This is based on the work of one of our research students (Venkat Rao, 1995). This village has a high proportion of Scheduled Castes population in the total population in 1991. At this time, Scheduled Castes population constituted 41.8% of the total population and Scheduled Tribes constituted 1.2% of the total population. The village has 1249 total households, including 522 Scheduled Castes households. Of the rest, 526 households were landless; 77% of which belonged to Scheduled Castes while the rest belonged to other castes. The marginal farmers among Scheduled Castes were only 21.77%, whereas in the case of others they formed 44.56%. The cultivators were more concentrated (i.e. 20.17%) among other castes, but only 8.11% were among Scheduled Castes. Scheduled Castes, who constituted more than 40% of the total population, controlled only 183 acres of land (i.e. 8%), while others, who constituted about 60% of the population, controlled 2,100 acres of land (i.e. 92% of total land).

The occupational distribution of the village shows the predominance of agricultural labourers, which constitute 55.25% of the total workforce. Out of the total population, 48.41% were workers. Of the total workforce, the Scheduled Castes workers constituted around 59%, while other castes constituted 41.69%. Among Scheduled Castes workers, agricultural labourers constituted 79.05% as against 33.84% among the other castes and 55.25% in the total village.

It was also found that 91.04% of the Scheduled Castes female workers are agricultural labourers. To study the change in the structure of the labour force, a sample of 100 agricultural labour households with heads above 35 years age was selected randomly in this village. The required information was collected by enquiring about their past history and their present positions. The total population of the sample of 100 (70 SCs + 30 others) agricultural labour households was 528, comprising 49.25% males and 50.75% females. The population of Scheduled Castes constituted 69.32% (366) of the total population, of whom 174 were men (66.93% of the total male population) and192 (71.64% of the total female population) were women. Other castes constituted 30.68% (i.e. 162) of which 33.07% (86) were males and 28.36% (76) were females. It was found that out of 30 labour households of other castes, nine households have less than two acres of farming land and three households have three acres each. But in the case of Scheduled Castes, all 70 labour households were landless and are depending on agricultural labour for their livelihood. Of the total sample population of 528, literates were 211, constituting 39.96% of people in the village. Among the Scheduled Castes, the literacy rate was only 36%, while it was 49% among other castes.

Of the 100 household heads in the sample, 88% of them started their lives as 'Palerulu' (attached labourers). Of 70 Scheduled Castes households, 67 household heads (i.e. 95.27%) worked as Palerulu in 1964–1965 or before. Of the 30 other caste households 21 heads (i.e. 70%) worked as Palerulu. Similarly, of 70 household heads of Scheduled Castes 67 persons (i.e. 95.72%) worked as Palerulu before 1964–1965. Furthermore, 21 (i.e. 31.34% of them) gave it up before 1974–1975 and about 42 (i.e. 62.68% of them) left it after 1974–1975. But in 1993–1994, four household heads were still working as Palerulu. Whereas in the case of other castes, out of 30 households heads 21 labourers (that is, 70% of the sample) worked as Palerulu before 1964–1985. Apart from this, 16 (i.e. 76.20% of them) gave it up before 1974–1975 and the remaining household heads left it after 1974–1975. But only one household head was working as Palerulu in 1993–1994. This person entered the contract of attached labour due to the reasons like the wedding of his two daughters. It was also found that in 1993–1994 among Scheduled Castes about 5 children below 14 years were working as cattle boys, which could not be found in other Castes. Thus, the proportion of attached labourers was high before 1974–1975, but declined significantly by 1993–1994.

Debt clearance after marriage, and labour migration to the urban areas, changed wage payments from in kind to cash, the low level of wage rate of attached labourers compared to the casual wage rate, the differential treatment of attached labourers by farmers on the basis of social hierarchy, decline in perquisites, and the increasing costs of cattle have been found to be important reasons for change in the composition of labourers, i.e. change of attached labourers into casual labourers.

From the above analysis of Malkapalli village, it also follows that land concentration continues in the hands of the upper castes in 1993–1994. Although the degree of attached labour declined substantially, Scheduled Caste workers principally remained as agricultural labourers and child labour continued in case of Scheduled Castes workers to some extent.

In the light of the above analysis, one can conclude that the process of change that has been initiated through land legislation, new technology and other developmental measures could not bring any significant change in the socio-economic conditions of Scheduled Castes. There was no improvement in their asset position in terms of land. Although there was a change in the structure of Scheduled Caste workers, that is, attached labourers were converted into casual labourers, they essentially remained as agricultural labourers.

It is also to be noted that the studies on poverty established that the incidence of poverty is higher in agricultural labourers. In the cases of SCs, the incidence of rural poverty was 43.5% and urban poverty was 33.0%, while in the case of others the incidence of rural poverty was 33.8% and urban poverty was 20.9% in 2009–2010 at the all-India level (Statistical Profile of Scheduled Tribes in India 2013; Ministry of Tribal Affairs Statistics Division Government of India, 2010, p. 94). These poorer groups, particularly Dalit agricultural labourers are, often subject to atrocities committed by land owning castes.

6.5 Atrocities against Dalits

According to the report of the Commission of SCs/STs there are three main reasons for the commission of atrocities against them: (1) unresolved land disputes related to the allocation of government land or distribution of surplus land to the landless SC/ST persons: (2) tensions and bitterness created on account of the non-payment or underpayment of minimum wages prescribed by the State government; and (3) resentment against manifestation of awareness among the Scheduled Castes and Scheduled Tribes about their rights and privileges as enshrined in the constitution and various legislative and executive measures. Despite these measures, there was a steady raise in the number of atrocities on Scheduled Castes/Scheduled Tribes persons from 1981–2014 at the all-India level (Tables 6.4–6.7). It also observed

Table 6.4 Statement showing the number of IPC crimes against members of the Scheduled Castes at the all-India level

Year	*Murder*	*Rape*	*Kidnaps*	*Dacoity*	*Robbery*	*Arson*	*Hurt*	*PCRact*	*POAact*	*Others*	*Total*
1981	493	604	NA	NA	NA	1295	1492	NA	NA	10434	14318
1986	564	727	NA	NA	NA	1002	1408	NA	NA	11715	15416
1991	610	784	NA	NA	NA	602	1706	NA	NA	13944	17646
1996	543	949	NA	NA	NA	464	4585	NA	NA	24899	31440
2001	763	1316	400	41	133	354	4547	633	13113	12201	33501
2002	739	1331	319	29	105	322	4491	1018	10770	14383	33507
2003	581	1089	232	24	70	204	3969	634	8048	11401	26252
2004	654	1157	253	26	72	211	3824	364	8891	11435	26827
2005	669	1172	258	26	80	210	3847	291	8497	11077	26127
2006	673	1217	280	30	90	226	3760	405	8581	11808	27070
2007	674	1349	332	23	86	238	3814	206	9819	13490	30031
2008	626	1457	482	51	85	225	4216	248	11602	14623	33615
2009	624	1346	512	44	70	195	4410	168	11143	15082	33594
2010	570	1349	511	42	75	150	4376	143	10513	14983	32712
2011	673	1557	616	36	54	169	4247	67	11342	14958	32712
2012	651	1576	490	27	40	214	3855	62	12576	14164	33719
2013	676	2073	628	45	62	189	4901	62	13975	16797	33655
2014											

Sources: 1. Reports of the Commissioner of SC/ST (1986–1987), p. 238.

2. Various Reports of NCRD, Government of India.

Table 6.5 Statement showing the number of IPC crimes against members of the Scheduled Tribes at the all-India level

Years	*Murder*	*Rape*	*Kidnapping*	*Dacoity*	*Robbery*	*Arson*	*Hurt*	*Act*	*SC&ST(POA)*	*Others*	*Total*
1981	110	259	-	-	-	46	260	-	-	2657	3432
1982	133	256	-	-	-	132	320	-	-	3261	4102
1983	161	262	-	-	-	238	310	-	-	3163	4134
1984	171	312	-	-	-	132	348	-	-	3327	4290
1985	148	243	-	-	-	198	323	-	-	3143	4055
1986	160	285	-	-	-	232	311	-	-	2957	3945
2005	164	640	72	27	49	38	767	162	1283	2511	5713
2006	195	699	88	12	29	46	838	49	1232	2603	5791
2007	140	627	89	9	21	54	855	5	1104	2628	5532
2008	128	585	93	14	18	49	875	6	1022	2794	5582
2009	118	583	82	3	24	29	787	2	944	3853	5425
2010	142	654	84	7	5	39	941	5	1169	2839	5885
2011	143	772	137	7	9	24	803	7	1154	2700	5756
2012	156	729	103	5	15	26	816	2	1311	2759	5922
2013	122	847	130	8	7	33	930	25	1390	3301	6793
2014											

Sources: 1. Reports of the Commissioner of SC/ST (1986–1987), p. 238.

2. Various Reports of Crime in India, NCRD, Government of India.

Table 6.6 Statement showing the number of cases of crimes against the Scheduled Castes committed by members of non-Scheduled Castes in the various states and UTs during 1991–2014

	1991	*1998*	*1999*	*2000*	*2001*	*2010*	*2011*	*2012*	*2013*	*2014*
Andhra Pradesh	660	565	522	529	612	4271	4006	3048	3264	2104
Arunachal Pradesh	-	-	-	-	-	0	0	0	0	0
Assam	14	-	-	1	-	7	0	4	8	2
Bihar	551	269	276	220	169	3516	3623	4821	6721	7874
Chhattisgarh	-	-	-	48	48	340	253	262	242	359
Goa	5	-	1	1	4	1	4	9	11	12
Gujarat	1101	595	415	211	152	1008	1061	1026	1190	1075
Haryana	68	18	18	19	31	380	408	252	493	444
Himachal Pradesh	25	19	21	16	36	100	91	126	144	113
Jharkhand	-	-	-	-	-	0	0	696	978	903
Karnataka	732	902	1131	1073	1129	577	636	2594	2555	1865
Kerala	650	297	194	146	163	2472	2473	810	756	712
Madhya Pradesh	5432	401	433	539	440	583	760	2875	2945	3294
Maharashtra	537	141	160	128	120	3373	3245	1086	1657	1763
Manipur	-	-	-	-	-	1107	1133	0	1	1
Meghalaya	-	-	-	-	-	0	0	0	0	0
Mizoram	-	-	-	-	-	0	0	0	0	0
Nagaland	-	-	-	-	-	0	0	0	0	0
Odisha	362	227	263	147	306	0	0	2265	2592	1657
Punjab		6	6	13	15	1707	1455	71	126	123
Rajasthan	2098	958	887	454	818	115	90	5559	6475	6734
Sikkim	-	-	-	-	-	4979	5177	5	6	3
Tamil Nadu	-	300	366	418	305	3	9	1638	1844	1486
Telangana	-	-	-	-	-	1628	1379	-	-	1427
Tripura	553	-	-	-	-	11	22	76	48	1
Uttar Pradesh	4798	2737	2597	2683	3318	6272	7702	6201	7078	8066
Uttarakhand		-	-	-	-	35	32	33	34	60
West Bengal	9	-	-	-	1	63	59	85	115	130
A & N Islands	-	-	-	-	-	0	0	0	0	0
Chandigarh	-	-	-	-	1	0	2	2	4	1
Dadra &Nagar Haveli	1	-	-	-	-	0	1	0	0	0
Daman & Diu	-	-	-	-	1	0	0	0	1	0
Delhi	6	8	10	12	7	16	28	44	52	86
Lakshadweep	-	-	-	-	-	0	0	0	0	0
Puducherry	5	-	2	4	-	5	3	4	6	5
Total	17646	7445	7301	6615	7710	32569	33652	33592	39346	40300

Sources: 1. Reports of the Commissioner of SC/ST (2004–2005), p. 238.

2. Various Reports of Crime in India, NCRD, Government of India.

Table 6.7 Statement showing the number of cases of atrocities against the Scheduled Tribes committed by members of non-Scheduled Tribes during 1991–2014

	1991	*1998*	*1999*	*2000*	*2001*	*2010*	*2011*	*2012*	*2013*	*2014*
Andhra Pradesh	129	64	39	83	99	803	802	666	672	389
Arunachal Pradesh	-	-	-	-	-	54	34	10	1	0
Assam	6	-	-	-	-	3	2	0	0	1
Bihar	14	73	14	15	1	71	97	119	91	77
Chhattisgarh	-	-	-	-	30	507	336	344	331	475
Goa	-	1	-	-	-	0	1	1	9	6
Gujarat	203	55	45	16	9	155	153	221	224	223
Haryana	-	2	-	-	-	0	0	0	0	0
Himachal Pradesh	3	1	-	-	1	2	4	3	2	3
Jharkhand	-	-	-	-	-	0	0	287	396	402
Karnataka	46	35	49	44	59	234	309	373	521	397
Kerala	102	25	14	7	12	294	281	124	135	120
Madhya Pradesh	3265	85	105	146	172	88	231	1218	1296	1577
Maharashtra	285	31	18	13	19	1383	1284	307	407	443
Manipur	-	-	-	-	-	292	321	2	2	1
Meghalaya	-	-	-	-	-	0	1	0	0	1
Mizoram	-	-	-	-	-	0	0	0	0	1
Nagaland	-	-	-	-	-	0	0	0	18	0
Odisha	164	91	94	34	88	0	0	688	790	533
Punjab		-	4	1	4	556	484	0	0	0
Rajasthan	539	213	175	54	126	0	0	1351	1651	1681
Sikkim		1	-	-	-	1319	1263	4	17	1
Tamil Nadu	-	7	11	4	-	1	8	27	23	18
Telangana	-	-	-	-	--	33	23	-	-	333
Tripura	-	-	-	-	-	35	30	29	24	0
Uttar Pradesh	-	40	6	11	7	0	35	44	25	24
Uttarakhand	-	-	-	-	-	0	0	3	2	1
West Bengal	8	-	-	-	1	47	41	91	122	107
A & N Islands	-	-	-	-	-	1	7	4	1	6
Chandigarh	-	-	-	-	-	0	0	0	0	0
Dadra &Nagar Haveli	6	1	-	-	-	2	2	4	7	3
Daman & Diu	-	-	-	-	-	0	0	0	1	0
Delhi	-	-	-	-	-	0	0	0	0	0
Lakshadweep	-	-	-	1	-	0	0	0	0	0
Puducherry	-	-	-	-	-	0	0	0	0	1
Total	4778	725	574	432	628	5880	5749	5920	6768	6824

Sources: 1. Reports of the Commissioner of SC/ST (2004–2005), p. 238.

2. Various Reports of Crime in India, NCRD, Government of India.

that the number of atrocities on Scheduled Castes/Scheduled Tribes also increased (1991–2014) at the state level.

The dispute over wages and the occupation of land have been at the root of recurrent killings of Dalits when Dalits try to take the possession of the land allotted to them by government and when Dalit agricultural workers insist on the payment of minimum wages as fixed by the government (Report of the Commissioner for SCs and STs 1986–1987, p. 238). As explained above, the inequalities in the distribution of land is persisting due to the failure of land reforms in India and this iniquitous agrarian structure gives rise to tension between different classes leading to atrocities on Dalits. And atrocities are being committed against these SC/ST groups by others, particularly landowning castes.

The following is also noted from a report *Broken People: Caste Violence against India's "Untouchables* by Human Rights Watch, published in New York, March 1999.

In the late 1980s, in Chenaganambatti village in Madurai district, Tamil Nadu, 95 acres of idle land belonging to a temple under the Hindu Religious Endowment Act were auctioned and sold to villagers for cultivation. At that time, some 5,00,000 acres of such idle land existed in Tamil Nadu. Caste Hindus did not allow Dalits to take part in the auction. In 1989 Dalits began demanding participation and, in 1992, finally succeeded in entering the auction. Caste Hindus protested and appealed to the Commissioner of the Hindu Religious Endowment Act, a Central Government official. The commissioner decreed that the lands bought at auction actually belonged to the Dalits. One month later, and in broad daylight, one hundred members of the Kallar community, an upper-caste group, invaded and destroyed nine acres of paddy (rice) fields belonging to Dalits. In subsequent attacks, the Kallars murdered two Dalit men and assaulted three Dalit women, who sustained head injuries. Between 1994 and 1999, a total of 98,349 cases were registered nationwide with the police as crimes and atrocities against Scheduled Castes. Of these, 38,483 were registered under the Atrocities Act. A further 1,660 were for murder, 2184 for rape and 13, 671 for hurt (*Broken People: Caste Violence against India's "Untouchables*", Human Rights Watch, New York, March 1999, p. 41).

It is also to be noted that in backward states such as Bihar atrocities against Dalits have been increasing in recent times, with most of these being connected with issues surrounding land and minimum wages. Bihar has the highest number of very large landholders and one of the largest landless population among all Indian states. "Disparities in socio-economic hierarchy run alongside the caste hierarchy throughout Bihar although the degree of relationship may differ in some districts. Scheduled Castes invariably fall in the lowest category both socially and economically" (ibid., pp. 42–43).

Various upper-caste senas began to emerge in Bihar with the reported aim of containing Naxalite groups and protecting the land belonging to upper castes. On September 27, 1991 the Bhumihar-dominated Savarna Liberation Front came into existence in 1990 was responsible for many massacres.

On September 27, 1991 the Sena beheaded seven Dalits and tribal labourers in Swanibigha Village in Jehnabad district. Soon thereafter strongmen hired by landlords in Teendiha Village in Gaya District beheaded nine labourers for their refusal to work as farmhands for paltry wages (ibid., pp. 42–48). On December 1, 1997 in the Village of Laxmanpur, Bathe, Jehnabad District, Bihar the Ranavira Sena, a militia of upper-caste landlords shot dead 61 Dalits:16 children, 27 women and 18men. Five of the victims, teenage girls, were raped and mutilated before being shot in the chest. The villagers were reportedly sympathetic to a Marxist-Leninist (Naxalite) group that had been demanding more equitable land distribution in the area (ibid., p. 49). The same source reported that the Ranavira Sena has been responsible for the massacre of more than 400 Dalit villagers in Bihar between 1995 and 1999 (ibid., p. 4).

6.6 Summary and conclusion

The individual cases in Tamil Nadu and Bihar illustrated above clearly indicate linkages between caste, land and labour and social tensions in rural areas, resulting in the violation of constitutionally guaranteed human rights of Dalits who are mostly landless agricultural labourers. The iniquitous distribution pattern of land and associated feudalism was mostly responsible for frequent physical attacks on Dalits (agricultural labourers) in rural India. To remove those inequalities and resolve the problem of social tensions and violation of human rights strict implementation of land reform and redistribution of land among Dalit agricultural labourers is highly warranted. State intervention in the form of protecting Dalits' Rights, strict implementation of legislative measures and anti-poverty programmes should also be strengthened. State should expand educational facilities to agricultural workers, particularly to landless Dalit agricultural labourers, to improve their skills so that they need not depend on landlords for their livelihood and they will be in a position to shift to non-farm employment. The problems of social tensions and the violation of human rights recurs as long as the agrarian structure remains iniquitous in the rural economy and agricultural labourers continue to depend on landlords for their livelihood.

References

Government of India. (1986–1987). *Report of the Commissioner for SCs and STs*. New Delhi, pp. 238–240.

Government of India. (2010). *Statistical Profile of Scheduled Tribes in India*. Ministry of Tribal Affairs, Statistics Division, Government of India, New Delhi, p. 107. www.tribal.nic.in.

Government of India. (2013). *Statistical Profile of Scheduled Tribes in India 2013*. Ministry of Tribal Affairs Statistics Division Government of India, New Delhi, p. 94.

Government of Maharashtra, Education Department. (1989. *Dr.Ambedkar's Writings and Speeches*, Vol. 5, p. 94.

Human Rights Watch. (1999). *Broken People: Caste Violence Against India's "Untouchables"*. New York, USA, March, ISBN 1-56432-228-9.

Nancharaiah, G. (1990). The changing position of scheduled caste as agricultural labourers in the labour market. *Social Action (New Delhi)*, 40(2), pp. 172–183.

National Sample Survey Organisation. (2013). *Household's Ownership Holdings and Operational Holding*. Ministry of Statistics and Programme Implementation, Government of India, New Delhi, Report No 571, 70th round, January–December, p. 28.

Venkat Rao, G. (1995). New technology and its impact on agricultural labour institutions: A study of a village in Coastal Andhra. M.Phil. dissertation submitted to, School of Economics University of Hyderabad, Hyderabad.

Index

Page numbers in **bold** refer to tables; *italics* refer to figures

For Product Safety Concerns and Information please contact our EU
representative GPSR@taylorandfrancis.com
Taylor & Francis Verlag GmbH, Kaufingerstraße 24, 80331 München, Germany

www.ingramcontent.com/pod-product-compliance
Ingram Content Group UK Ltd.
Pitfield, Milton Keynes, MK11 3LW, UK
UKHW020000200926
475702UK00015B/2398

* 9 7 8 0 3 6 7 7 0 5 8 2 4 *